VGM Careers for You Series

W9-AGI-367

CAREERS FOR

MYSTERY BUFFS

& Other
Snoops and Sleuths

Blythe Camenson

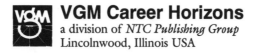

VGM Career Horizons
a division of *NTC Publishing Group*
Lincolnwood, Illinois USA

To my friend Chris, a master of mystery and intrigue.

Library of Congress Cataloging-in-Publication Data

Camenson, Blythe.
    Careers for mystery buffs / Blythe Camenson
        p. cm.
    Includes bibliographical references.
        ISBN 0-8442-4331-0 (alk. paper). —ISBN 0-8442-4332-9 (pbk. :
    alk. paper)
        1. Authorship—Vocational guidance. 2. Authorship—Handbooks,
    manual, etc. 3. Vocational guidance. 4. Mystery and detective
    stories—Handbooks, manuals, etc. I. Title.
    PN151.C278 1996
    331.7'02—dc20   96-2034
                                                        CIP

Published by VGM Career Horizons, a division of NTC Publishing Group
4255 West Touhy Avenue
Lincolnwood (Chicago), Illinois 60646-1975, U.S.A.
©1997 by NTC Publishing Group. All rights reserved.
No part of this book may be reproduced, stored in a retrieval
system, or transmitted in any form or by any means,
electronic, mechanical, photocopying, recording or otherwise,
without the prior permission of NTC Publishing Group.
Manufactured in the United States of America.

567890VP987654321

Contents

About the Author

Ever since she read her first *Nancy Drew*, Blythe Camenson has been a die-hard mystery fan. Combining that with her love of writing suspense novels and her position as director of Fiction Writer's Connection made this book a natural choice for her to write.

A full-time writer of career books, Blythe Camenson's main concern is helping job seekers make educated choices. She firmly believes that with enough information, readers can find long-term, satisfying careers. To that end she researches traditional as well as unusual occupations, talking to a variety of professionals about what their jobs are really like. In all of her books, she includes first-hand accounts from people who can reveal what to expect in each occupation.

Camenson was educated in Boston, earning her B.A. in English and psychology from the University of Massachusetts and her M.Ed. in counseling from Northeastern University.

In addition to *Careers for Mystery Buffs*, Camenson has written more than a dozen career guidance books for VGM Career Horizons.

Acknowledgments

The author would like to thank the following mystery buffs for providing information about their careers:

Kent Brinkley
Landscape Architect/Garden
  Historian
Colonial Williamsburg
Williamsburg, Virginia

Tim Bronson
Detective Sergeant
Fort Lauderdale Police
  Department
Fort Lauderdale, Florida

Matthew Carone
Art Gallery Owner
Fort Lauderdale, Florida

Robyn Carr
Suspense Writer
Tempe, Arizona

Carol Soret Cope
True Crime Writer
Miami, Florida

Dianne Ell
President
Mystery Writers of America,
Florida Chapter
Deerfield Beach, Florida

John Fleckner
Chief Archivist
National Museum of
  American History
Smithsonian Institution
Washington, D.C.

Connie Gay
Producer
MurderWatch
Orlando, Florida

Noreen Grice
Education Coordinator/
  Astronomer
Charles Hayden Planetarium
Museum of Science
Boston, Massachusetts

David Kaufelt
Mystery Writer
Key West, Florida

Kristin Kuckelman
Field Archaeologist
Crow Canyon Archaeological
  Center
Cortez, Colorado

Bob Lemons
Fire Investigator
Boca Raton, Florida

Nancy McVicar
Investigative Reporter
Sun-Sentinel
Fort Lauderdale, Florida

Joe Nickell
Paranormal Investigator
Committee for the Scientific
    Investigation of Claims of
    the Paranormal (CSICOP)
Center for Inquiry
Amherst, New York

Ramesh Nyberg
Homicide Detective
Metro-Dade Police
Miami, Florida

Larry Schindler
Director
Charles Hayden Planetarium
Museum of Science
Boston, Massachusetts

Patricia Sprinkle
Publicity Chairperson
Sisters in Crime
Lawrence, Kansas

Al Sunshine
Investigative Reporter
WCIX
Miami, Florida

Carolyn Travers
Director of Research
Plimoth Plantation
Plymouth, Massachusetts

CHAPTER ONE

Jobs for Mystery Buffs

W
ho loves a good mystery? A lot of people do, it seems.
The popularity of thousands of detective books, police
procedurals, psychological suspense thrillers, and mysteries from "cozies" to "Regencies" can attest to that.

The program *Murder She Wrote* kept fans glued to the television
set on Sunday nights for years. Even a change in the viewing slot
couldn't hurt ratings. Slews of other mystery and police shows—
NYPD Blue, Columbo, Perry Mason, Law and Order, to name just a
few—keep viewers entertained nightly.

The number of professional writers publishing mystery books
each year—membership in Mystery Writers of America hovers in
the thousands—seems to almost equal the number of readers. An
even higher figure encompasses all those new writers striving to
break in and get their first book published.

But it's not just readers, TV viewers, and writers who enjoy a
good puzzle. Anyone who has ever successfully utilized deductive
and analytic skills to solve a problem or find the answer to a question
knows the satisfaction of a job well done.

An even better satisfaction comes from being able to combine
those skills and a love of a good mystery in a rewarding, full-time
career.

Do You Have What It Takes?

If you've got this book in hand, you already know you're a mystery
buff. But an armchair mystery fan doesn't necessarily have all the

skills needed to be out there in the field, digging, probing, researching, investigating, and solving a variety of problems.

Before we investigate career options that would appeal to mystery buffs, let's see if you have what it takes. Are any of the following statements true for you?

— You're the first to grab the Sunday crossword puzzle each week.

— You were able to track down an old friend you lost touch with years ago.

— You've done all the research on your family tree.

— You ask a lot of questions. (Some people think you're nosy.)

— You strive to understand what makes people tick.

— The behavior of your dog or cat fascinates you.

— You love listening to gossip (but you never indulge in it yourself).

— You're curious about events around you.

— You're not satisfied until you know *why* something happened.

— You're not satisfied until you know *how* something happened.

— You love learning something new.

— You're not afraid of acquiring a new skill. (Computers don't make you cringe.)

— Poring through old records and dusty reference books seems like heaven to you.

— You refuse to quit until you've found the answers you're looking for.

If you were able to put a checkmark next to at least ten of the fourteen statements, then read on. In the following pages you'll find a career where you can put your talents and interests to good use.

Investigating Career Options

Mystery buffs find careers in a variety of traditional and innovative settings. Some will be very familiar to you; others will spark ideas and give you new areas to consider.

What follows is an overview of general categories. You can learn more about each career in the chapters ahead.

Becoming a Mystery Writer

What mystery buff wouldn't love to see his or her own creation, neatly bound in hardcover with a glossy jacket, proudly displayed in a bookstore window? Is it just a dream, or could it really happen? Learn how mystery writers journey through the different stages from idea to publication and how you can follow in their footsteps.

A Nose for News

Mystery buffs with a flair for words and a nose for news work at newspapers and television stations. Do you love to snoop? Could you uncover a scam? Expose a crook? Right a wrong? If so, then you could find satisfying work as an investigative reporter.

The World of Crime

Perhaps writing isn't your thing. You'd much rather be out there in the thick of it, tracking criminals and bringing them to justice. Law enforcement personnel—homicide and robbery detectives, FBI and DEA agents, private investigators, arson investigators, criminologists, attorneys, and a score of others—all use their wits to solve crimes, prosecute offenders, defend clients, and see to it that the justice system works.

Unsolved Mysteries

Do you believe in ESP? Life after death? UFOs? Parapsychologists are interested in reports of hauntings, sightings of unidentified flying objects, and any other type of paranormal activity. Paranormal psychologists investigate the same phenomena and try to eliminate obvious explanations.

Mysteries of the Past

There are several careers suited to mystery buffs who have a love of history. Historians work in a variety of settings: in living history museums, universities, or libraries; for historical societies; or for architectural firms. Archaeologists travel to faraway sites, literally uncovering the past one grain of sand at a time. Landscape archaeologists use traditional archaeological techniques to uncover gardens that might have existed on a site in a given historical period. Genealogists act as detectives to the past, tracing missing persons and filling in the holes in family histories. Archivists provide a service to society by identifying and preserving materials with lasting value for the future. Researchers work in living history museums to recreate period characters or to find information to help restore historic buildings.

Mysteries of the Mind

Mystery buffs intrigued with the intricacies of the human mind can pursue a variety of psychology specialties, including abnormal, experimental, developmental, educational, and social psychology. These research psychologists study behavior, how people develop and learn, and how they react in certain situations.

Mysteries of the Universe

For some, nothing is more intriguing than the mysteries of the universe. To understand our origins they look to the heavens, to our plant life and environment, and to the depths of the oceans. They work in museums, planetariums, libraries, botanical gardens, and marine biology laboratories.

Although all these careers have distinct differences, they also have some elements in common; each professional working in any of the above-mentioned fields relies on intelligence, logic, and persistence to uncover, dig up, research, investigate, examine, probe, and explore a variety of issues specific to his or her particular job.

The Qualifications You'll Need

Because the careers in which mystery buffs can exercise their investigative talents vary so greatly, it is understandable that so will the requirements and qualifications for employment. More and more professional jobs require at least a bachelor's degree. However, there are some professions highlighted here that expect applicants to have certain specialized skills rather than diplomas.

Below is a chart listing many of the careers featured in the following pages. Pinpoint the job that interests you, then look to the right-hand columns to find the education or training requirements. Each job's prerequisites will be covered more fully in the chapters ahead.

Job Title	High School	BA/BS	MA/MS	PhD	Other
		Requirements			
Writer					X
Investigative Reporter	R				
Private Investigator					X
Police Detective					R
Attorney					
Archaeologist		R	P		R
Archivist		R	P		
Genealogist					X
Astronomer		R	P		
Botanist		R	P		
Psychologist			R		
Parapsychologist					X
Paranormal Investigator					X

P = Preferred; R = Required; X = needed but not required in terms of official degrees or credentials

Salaries

Just as the required qualifications differ, so do salaries. How much you'll earn will depend on your work setting, your employer, your level of education and training, and also the geographic area in which you live. Throughout the following chapters you will learn more about the specific salaries professionals in each featured career can expect to draw.

Whodunit?

Becoming a Mystery Writer

A lthough writers come from all sorts of backgrounds and are as different from one person to the next, they do share a few things in common. Writers love words, They love how they sound and feel and how they fit together in original and rhythmic ways.

Mystery writers combine their love of words with a love of puzzles. Whereas some mystery buffs enjoy solving these puzzles, mystery writers prefer to create and build them.

Becoming a professional writer is not an easy task, however. The new writer faces stiff competition from experienced writers with proven track records. Impersonal rejection slips become a way of life for the new writer, who sometimes must wonder if there's a better shot at winning the lottery than getting published.

But new writers do get published every year (a lot more than lucky lottery winners). It takes a lot of persistence, and a little luck, but if it's what you want more than anything else, you *can* make it happen.

Do You Have What It Takes?

Mystery writers are creative, imaginative people. After all, they have to be; they make up stories for a living. They have to be able to create imaginary characters and events and make them seem real to their readers.

Mystery writers have to be troublemakers, too, inventing all sorts of problems for their characters. They have to make characters' conversations and thoughts entertaining and fill their lives with action. Finally, fiction writers have to be expert problem solvers, helping their heroes find satisfying solutions to their troubles by the end of the story.

If you love to read mysteries and you find yourself stopping in the middle of a book and saying out loud, "I could do that better," then maybe you can.

Here are seven tips to guide you down the road to success.

1. Don't Give Up Your Day Job— The Financial Realities of the Writing Profession

Few new fiction writers have the luxury of working at their craft full-time. Most need to maintain some other sort of employment to help pay the bills until they are able to support themselves through their writing.

Even if you manage to break in and sell your first novel, you should expect to receive an advance of about $2500 to $5000. The six-figure advances that some superstar authors receive are not the norm. Zebra Books senior editor John Scognamiglio says, "That kind of stuff like with John Grisham doesn't really have anything to do with the rest of us. There are 110,000 new titles a year, and there are only fifteen on the *New York Times* best-seller list at a time. Most of the rest of us are going to make a moderate income and do a civilized business if we work very, very hard. There's not that much room at the top. And there isn't much of a middle class in publishing. You either make a little bit of money, which the grand majority will do, or you make a lot."

If you do manage to land that first book contract, you will receive an advance against royalties. A royalty is a percentage, usually 6 to

10 percent, of the money your book earns in sales. The advance is usually paid half on signing the contract, half on deliverance and acceptance of the manuscript.

Other perks include recognition and publicity, though some might view the attention as a downside. Many writers report that the nicest perk is being able to go to work in their bathrobe.

2. Read, Read, Read

If you want to write mysteries, you have to be completely familiar with the genre. You can't just decide, "Well, mysteries are popular and they sell well, so I guess that's what I'll write." If you don't know the category, including all the rules and all the ins and outs, it will show in your writing.

Literary agent Nancy Yost advises new writers to read, read, and read some more. "It's important to read other writers, and to know what other people are reading. The best writers are avid readers."

Agent Pesha Rubenstein adds to that advice. "Read a lot, but not just the established writers, such as Danielle Steel or Stephen King. Read everything current; read the new authors that are being put out now. This is the kind of material publishers are looking for."

3. Know the Market

You have to know what's out there: what's being published, what's being read. Although you want your book to be fresh and original, it can't veer so far from the established norm that no publisher will want to take a chance with it.

"Know the market," says Frank Walgren, editor at Leisure Books. "Know what publishers are looking for before you go about submitting anything—before you even go about writing anything."

4. Make the Time to Write

Dedicated writers use every spare minute they have to work on their books or stories. John Grisham, for example, wrote a good deal of *The Firm* on yellow legal pads while taking the train to and from work as a full-time attorney in a law firm.

Others get up an hour earlier, stay up an hour later, turn down invitations to parties or other social events, or let the housework go—whatever they can do to find the time to write.

Successful authors who support themselves through their writing treat it as a full-time job. Most report learning how to discipline themselves to put in a certain number of hours each day.

Every writer chooses a schedule that is comfortable to him or her. Some work in the early hours of the morning, take afternoon naps, and then go back to the computer in the evenings. Others write for eight or ten or twelve hours straight each day for months until the book is finished. Still others might take years to complete one volume.

There is no set formula for how a writer should work. The only rule is that you have to write. Author James Clavell said that even if you write only one page every day for a year, at the end of that time, you'll have 365 pages. And that's a good-sized book.

5. Hone Your Craft

How do you learn how to write or improve your writing skills? First, again, you must read. But as you're reading, don your detective's cap. Look for how the author has constructed the story. See how the plot twists and turns, and how it all ties together in the end. Examine the characters, study the dialogue, figure out what keeps you turning the pages. Then try to recreate that.

But you can't write in a vacuum. All writers need feedback. Many successful authors started out by participating in a small writer's group, meeting weekly and critiquing each other's work. Others attend seminars and workshops or take writing classes.

6. Know How to Submit Your Work

Writing a mystery novel is only half the battle. In addition to honing your skills as an expert storyteller, you also have to be a knowledge-able salesperson. That means you must learn which publishers you should approach and how to approach them. Several market guides that are mentioned at the end of this chapter will tell you what categories of fiction the different publishers buy. The guides will also list different magazines that purchase short stories. You can also check your own book collection to learn who the publishers are of your favorite mysteries and suspense books.

Once you've made a list of possible markets, you need to make sure your approach is appropriate. Your manuscript needs to be typed and double-spaced, with your name at the top of each page. There are several sources that can give you the information you need to format your manuscript properly.

Before you send in your completed manuscript, you should write the editor a brief letter describing your project. Include a one-page *synopsis*, or summary of your book's plot, and the first three chapters of your book as a sample. Don't forget to enclose an SASE, a self-addressed stamped envelope. The editor will use this to send you a reply. If the editor likes what he or she sees so far, you'll probably receive a request to send more.

Alternately you can look for an agent first, following the same steps you'd use to make your initial approach to a publisher. But here you are asking that the agent consider you as a possible client.

7. Keep Writing

After the query letters and sample chapters are in the mail, many new writers just sit back and wait for responses. The smart writer puts that manuscript out of mind and gets to work on the next one. And the next one. And the next one.

In the end the key to getting published can be summed up in one word: persistence.

John Grisham—A Success Story

John Grisham is an attorney turned writer. With six books to his credit at the time this book was written (*A Time to Kill, The Firm,*

The Pelican Brief, The Client, The Chamber, and *The Rainmaker*), several of which have been made into feature films, he is able to command very impressive advances. His first four books set a record by being on the best-seller list all at the same time.

But success didn't come quickly, or easily. First John had difficulty finding an agent to take him on; then when he had passed that hurdle, it took his agent a year to sell his first novel. A slew of rejection notices was finally replaced by the all-important acceptance—handed to him by Bill Thompson, an editor who is not afraid of promoting a newcomer. (He was the one who gave Stephen King his chance when no one else would, and published King's first novel, *Carrie.*) Bill paid John $15,000 for *A Time To Kill.* It came out in June 1989 with a print run of 5000. "I bought 1000, and another 1000 were sitting in a warehouse, so you know not many were out there," said John in an interview in *Publishers Weekly.*

Events progressed more rapidly with his second book, *The Firm.* A bootleg copy of his manuscript landed in the hands of Hollywood, and John was paid $600,000 for the movie rights by Paramount. And this was before a publisher had even seen the manuscript! Doubleday, one of the many houses that had passed on his first novel, then jumped at the chance to publish the book. "I still have the rejection letter," said John with a hint of a smile.

And he has a lot to be smiling about. There are now more than 20 million copies of his books in print.

Some Tips from Novelist Robyn Carr

Robyn Carr has written fourteen books since 1980, most in the historical romance or category romance genre. But recently she switched genres, and her latest book, *Mind Tryst,* is an excellent psychological suspense/woman-in-jeopardy thriller published by St. Martin's Press. Robyn also taught for the Writer's Digest School of Writing and is the author of *Practical Tips for Writing Popular Fiction* (Writer's Digest Books).

How did you get started writing?

I'm a very ordinary person. I've been married twenty-two years. I have a couple of kids—until recently I even drove a station wagon. While I was pregnant I read a lot and thought anybody with half a brain could do this, which is how everyone thinks in the beginning. You write that first book and you're sure it's going to be *Gone with the Wind*, but it's really junk. But something happens to you when you're doing it. It held my interest to the point that it became an obsessive desire to write. I couldn't wait to get back to it.

What was it like switching from romance to suspense?

I was scared to try at first, and then scared that I wasn't very good at it. I had spent twelve to fourteen years in romance; I had read everything that had been written, and I was getting burned-out. It was hard to find anything new. I was tired of writing it and tired of reading it. But I'm not tired of suspense—it's sort of like traveling. I've been through romance, now I'm in psychological suspense, and who knows where I'll go next.

How did you construct your plots?

There are so many things to remember when writing a suspense novel. I pass my manuscript through a couple of readers before I ever send it to my agent, and I get notes in the margins like, "Are we ever going to find out what happens to this?"

With romance I just use notes and simple 1-2-3, a-b-c outlines. But in suspense so much rests on when certain discoveries are made. I have to make plot outlines on index cards so that I can lay them out on the table and move them around. For example, at what point will Jackie discover things about Tom Wall in *Mind Tryst*? Or when does Jackie use the gun? One of the rules of writing is if you introduce a gun into a story you'd better use it. At some point during the writing of this book, I decided she had to have a gun, and I put that gun on index cards. "Gun hidden in laundry room closet." "Gun kept on the back of the toilet while she showers." I could put those index cards in certain places in the story and move them around. How these elements are arranged throughout the book is important to the reader.

How do you keep readers turning the pages?

A classic mistake made by new writers, and made by me so many times, is confusing building suspense with withholding information. But it's exactly the opposite. The more information you give, the more suspense you build.

Another problem with keeping secrets is that it breaks a hard-and-fast rule. If your main character, from whose viewpoint the story is written, knows something, the reader also has to know it. The information can be kept secret from other characters, but the reader is in her head and the character can't hide her thoughts from the reader.

The first rule of mystery is that your readers are entitled to an equal opportunity with your characters to solve the mystery.

Tell us about the writing process.

I was on a panel at a writer's conference, and someone who wanted to write a book stood up and asked, "What should you do? Should you force yourself to write the book from beginning to end; should you outline first; should you revise as you go along?" And everyone on the panel of six published authors—and some of them were very successful and making tons and tons of money—said that you should really outline first and force yourself to write through and then revise. However, I keep getting stuck going back to the beginning and revising and revising before I can carry on.

I have a real clear idea, before I begin, what's going to happen. Some minor things change, but the basic premise—who the bad guy is and how it's going to end—is real solid. I can't get past 50 pages without revising twenty times, and then I can't get past 100 pages without revising twenty times, and when I really hit my stride and the momentum takes me through to the end is at about 300 pages.

How do you develop your characters?

Until I've written an entire book, I'm not clear on what my characters' personalities are and how they feel about things. I'm always too passive in the first draft, reluctant to say, "Someone is so fat Omar the Tentmaker has to make her gown." I'll say that she's "overweight" or she's "a little on the chubby side." Or I give people emotions like "uncomfortable"—passive stuff—until I can finally get down and dirty about how they really feel. They're either angry or they're not, they're either scared or they're not—but they're not "uncomfortable."

Another problem is the expression, "She felt numb," or "She didn't know how she felt." Which usually means I don't know what she's feeling. But that won't work in fiction. The personality has to be clearly defined.

How did you make your first sale?

My first agent lived in San Antonio. He'd just opened the agency and was trying to build it up. He was my fourth or fifth attempt. I had been submitting things on my own before. I wrote query letters and killed myself hammering out synopses and revising the first three chapters 400 times. I would get the envelope ready for the next submission before the rejection came so I wouldn't be paralyzed with grief.

My agent made multiple copies and sent it to thirteen publishers—the thirteenth publisher took it. Avon, Bantam, and Berkley rejected it, and my heart was sinking lower and lower. I knew there was no hope; then Little, Brown and Company finally bought it, and I said, Little who? They are one of the finest publishers in America, but I hadn't heard of them. My first novel, *Chelynne*, was published in 1980.

Mystery Writer David Kaufelt

David Kaufelt, award-winning author of thirteen novels and the founder of the annual Key West Literary Seminar, has had a number of careers, including advertising ("Choosy Mothers Choose Jif") and teaching creative writing at Upsala College. (David also runs a mystery walking tour, which we'll learn about more in Chapter 8.) His first novel, *Six Months with an Older Woman*, was made into a television film starring John Ritter. *The Fat Boy Murders*, published by Pocket Books, is the first in a series of mysteries set in Sag Harbor, Long Island, featuring realtor detective Wynsome Lewis. The second in the series, *The Winter Women Murders*, debuted in 1994 and has been released in paperback. *Ruthless Realtor Murders* (Pocket Books) is the third in the series.

"I was in advertising when I started writing. My boss was a novelist, and I asked him, 'How do you get an idea?' Now I have about five million ideas and I can't imagine asking that question, but then I did. He said that he took an old novel that he really loved and used that plot. So I went back to my favorite novel, which was *Cheri*, by Colette. It's about a younger guy who's in love with an older woman. I switched it around, made it contemporary, and set it in New York. I spent the summer writing it in between writing commercials, but I was sort of pretending not to write it. I wrote it on the side because I was afraid. Fear is a big inhibitor. I finished it at the end of the summer and sent it to a famous agent. He eventually wrote back—his words are engraved in my heart, as you can imagine—'Dear Mr. Kaufelt, I can't do a thing with this, and neither can you.'

"I put the manuscript away for a while, then I sent it out to another agent, or two or three or ten, and finally one agent picked it up and she sold it very quickly. That was in 1971.

"I called my first book *Six Months with an Older Woman*. It did very well in hardcover and paper, and they wanted to make it into a movie in South America, but that never happened, for a variety of reasons. They wanted to pay me about twelve pesetas, for one.

"There was an actress, Estelle Parsons, who had read my book when she was at her beach house in California. We had met very briefly before—she had done a peanut butter commercial for us, actually. She wanted to know if she could take my book to two producers, and she wanted me to come along with her. We met in New York, and the producers liked the book very much. The next thing I knew was that Estelle was out and it was being made into a TV movie with John Ritter and an actress whose name escapes me right now. It was called *In Love with an Older Woman*, and it did very well. I had written this very good bagel of a book and they turned it into a BLT, but it was a very good BLT.

"I got a $5000 advance for the book and a lot of up-front money for the movie, about $50,000, but we're suing them now. The production house went bankrupt, and they never paid us the residuals for all the times it was shown on television. My agent is handling all that.

"*Bradley Beach Rumba*, my next book, came out in about 1973. It was a lovely book, the *New York Times* adored it, but it died a very quick death.

"Then I changed agents and wrote a book called *Spare Parts*, a medical thriller. It was an original paperback through Warner Books, and I got a hefty advance for that, about $60,000. Unfortunately it came out a few weeks after *Coma*, by Robin Cook. It would have been better if it had come out first, but it did very well. It made some of the regional best-seller lists. It's been optioned a couple of times, and it's now being optioned again for a television movie. How much you're going to get depends on how long the option is for. It could be between $5000 and $25,000.

"I wrote a big historical novel called *American Tropic*, which was a huge disappointment. The reviews were wonderful, but there were no sales. The publishing house hadn't backed it. I was very depressed when that happened. I had taken five years to research it, and I was very unhappy and ready to quit.

"But then a friend suggested I write a mystery because I like them so much. I had been reading them ever since I was a little boy, and I've really never stopped. There was a time when I was reading one a day. Some of my favorite authors are Agatha Christie, P.D. James, and Ngiao Marsh. I like English novels very much, and I really like Jane Austen. I find that 'little old lady' English mysteries are also social commentary, which is what my first books were— little comedies about society. And I was able to do this in *The Fat Boy Murders* and *The Winter Women Murders*.

"I think I didn't start writing mysteries right away because of prestige. There wasn't too much prestige associated with being a mystery writer then. Now I don't care. It's a very popular genre, but popularity doesn't necessarily make for prestige, although it's come a long way since I started writing.

"It took me a while to decide that mystery writing was what I wanted to do, and that it would be fun to do. But I haven't given up writing mainstream novels, either.

"When I started as a writer, it was extremely easy doing it. I loved doing it; I had a great time. I really like writing social comedy best, so the first two novels were easy; I just dashed them off. I've written some others like that. *Late Bloomers* is one. I think they have a reason for being. The hard ones, like *American Tropic*, which was five or six hundred pages and took all that research, wasn't fun, but it was very rewarding to do. I learned a great deal.

"At the beginning I wanted to make a name for myself very badly. Now publishers know who I am, certain readers know who I am, but that's not what I'm interested in these days. What I'm most interested in is my craft."

Some Advice from David Kaufelt

"I used to teach writing, and I had a kid who'd come in and I asked him, "Well, where's your work?" And he'd say, "Sorry, Professor Kaufelt, I wasn't inspired last night." But I don't think inspiration is where it's at. Writing as a craft is very hard work. You only get to do it better as you practice it. If you happen to be inspired and you happen to produce a work of genius, that's great, but that's not what I'm after. I'm honing my craft to be the best writer I can. I'm much more controlled than I used to be.

"It's good to have a great agent behind you. You should get an agent before you do anything else. Don't ever submit a book on your own without an agent. You could ask any publisher, and he'll probably tell you that 99 percent of the books that come in 'over the transom' are never read. If you happen to go to a publishing house where they read it then reject it, you can't resubmit the book there once you've found an agent. Maybe you sent it to the wrong editor, and there would have been another editor who was right to send your book to. That's what agents are good for, one hopes; getting it to the right person.

"I use my agents as pre-editors. I love for them to edit the book and tell me what they think. When you're a new writer, your book has to be as good as it can be before it goes out. Agents won't edit it for you. But for example, my newest book, *Ruthless Realtor Murders*, was already sold, so it behooves them to make it as good as they can.

"I always need a second person to look at my work, and not someone I'm associated with other than professionally. I don't want my best friend to look at it. I think it's really a mistake to let people who are not professionals tell you what they think of the book. They could give you the wrong advice, and you shouldn't care what they have to say. It doesn't matter. The only people I let tell me what to do are my agent and my editor.

"Writing is not an easy job. You have to be wonderfully self-disciplined. Even then it's not easy. I get up every morning at 6:00, get to the computer by 8:30, and I finish around 11:30 or noon. Then I go back in the late afternoon around 4:00 and work for another couple of hours. It's a good schedule. It gives me the middle of the day to think. But you know, I don't write my books when I'm at the computer, necessarily. I write them when I'm Rollerblading along the beach or doing something else.

"And people who say they don't have time to write their book, that they're waiting for the right moment—well, I don't believe that. That's all fear. All sorts of people had full-time jobs and still wrote. Joseph Heller was in advertising, for example. Advertising is a good place to work if you're on the creative side. It teaches you how to write succinctly.

"Finally: if you're going to take this road as a writer, you'd better have a day job."

Carol Soret Cope, True Crime Writer

When writing mysteries you are limited only by your imagination. When writing true crime you are bound by natural restraints; you are limited by the facts, by what actually happened. Occasionally an author can take liberal license, as Truman Capote did with *In Cold Blood*, which he contended was a "nonfiction novel." But for the most part you must stick to the true course of events.

The trick is in having your true crime book read just the way a mystery novel would. All the same elements must be present: suspense, conflict, character, and a fast pace. But you can't let yourself get too bogged down with the evidentiary material. You have to know how to structure your book, where to put what, and how to keep it interesting.

Carol Soret Cope is author of In the Fast Lane (Simon & Schuster, hardcover; St. Martin's Press, paperback), an account of the 1986 murder of wealthy Miami resident Stanley Cohen. Joyce Cohen, his fourth wife, was charged with the crime and later convicted.

"I'm a mediation lawyer. I'm not a criminal lawyer, and I had nothing to do with this case. But I was a partner in a large firm in downtown Miami. I live south of the city, and everyday I would drive the same route into work through Coconut Grove, a very picturesque suburb. I always noticed this one particular house, an older, very interesting house. It happened to be at a corner where there was a stoplight. I got stuck in traffic often, and I had plenty of time to observe this house. Because it was so evocative and in a mysterious setting, I used to wonder who the people were who lived there. But I didn't know them, and I never actually saw anybody there.

"Then one morning when I was driving to work, I saw yellow crime scene tape all around that particular house. There were emergency vehicles and TV news trucks there, so it was obvious something big had happened.

"I was very intrigued by what had happened in 'my' house, and in fact, it was the house where Stanley Cohen was murdered.

"I started following the story very carefully. It was a big story because the Cohen family was very well known. Stanley Cohen had been in Miami a long time and had a lot of friends and associates here. He'd been the owner of SAC Construction, a very successful company. His daughter is Gerri Helfman, a TV news anchor on the NBC affiliate in Miami. Joyce Cohen was something of a socialite. She drove a white Jaguar, wore designer clothes and lots of jewelry. They had their own yacht and their own plane, and they owned a big vacation ranch in Steamboat Springs, Colorado. They epitomized the good life in Miami in the eighties.

"I've always liked mystery fiction, crime fiction, and true crime, and this was the sort of story I'd always been interested in. I had read a lot of Ann Rule, the 'Queen of True Crime,' and one of her books that I had especially enjoyed was called *The Stranger Beside Me*. It's about Ted Bundy and the fact that she had worked side by side with him, trying to solve these crimes, not knowing that he was the one responsible.

"It was just chilling. To me the things that happen in real life are often more outrageous than anything we could ever make up, like with the O.J. Simpson case. Here's an affable, charming former athlete charged with those brutal murders. It's like the dark side of human nature.

"Years ago I was a high school English teacher, so I had always been interested in writing. And I always thought that one day I would write a book.

"I wanted to write about the Stanley Cohen case, but I didn't know where to start or what to do. I kept an eye on the case to see if it would develop to the point where there would be enough to make a book out of. That took several years.

"I waited until she'd been arrested. If no one was ever arrested for the crime, it would become an unsolved crime, and those aren't as marketable. I consulted Herman Klurfeld, who'd been Walter Winchell's ghostwriter. He's also the father of a friend of mine. He thought it was a good story, and he told me to get some information together so I could write a proposal and then get an agent. I did a lot of reading—you know, the Writer's Digest how-to books—and learned a lot about how to proceed and what to do. Herman helped put me in touch with an excellent agent, John Boswell. In fact, he's the author of a best-selling book, O.J.'s Legal Pad, a hilarious spoof on what O.J. was doodling and drawing in court. John took me on, and we went through two drafts of the book proposal. It was twenty pages long. Once that was done he got me a contract right away, with Simon & Schuster. The advance was substantial for an unknown author with a first book, and I was very pleased. Sales were very good; it was on the regional best-seller list for five weeks.

"I was supposed to write the book in a year, but it actually took me two and a half years. I started my research before I ever got the contract. The most important aspect was attending the trial every single day.

"What I would advise anybody interested in writing a true crime book is this: you can't do too much research before the trial. Try to pick the story before it goes to trial—and you can tell which ones are going to be big because they get a lot of news coverage—then go to the trial every day. A trial is like a play. You'll see or hear about all the characters that are important to the story. And you'll see them from both the prosecution's perspective and the defense's.

"You'll also get to meet these people after they've testified. Nobody wants to talk to you before. The witnesses won't talk to you, and neither will the attorneys or the cops, not until after the trial.

"What I did is, I sat in the courtroom and took voluminous notes. I didn't want to buy the trial transcript—which in this case cost about $10,000, and I didn't have a research budget. When witnesses got off the stand, I would run out to the hall, introduce myself, give them a business card, and ask if they'd be willing to talk to me when the trial was over. Many of them were rattled right after they'd testified and said they'd get back to me. But almost everyone I wanted to talk to got in touch with me after the verdict was in."

The Problem of Libel

"Libel is the big problem in true crime," Carol explains. "You need to rely on sworn statements; you rely on court testimony; you rely on depositions that were given under oath. This is the safe route to go, because then you have a person claiming that things happened a certain way under oath. It would be very difficult for him or her to later on come back and say, 'That didn't really happen that way, and you're libeling me by including that.'

"Another way to protect yourself, I've found, is to quote other people. Rather than having the author say, This character had shifty eyes and looked like a liar, you can have another character say it— that is, if someone did describe him that way or you're able to get someone to describe him that way. You put those words in somebody else's mouth, and that gives you one level of protection.

"There's another problem if you say, 'The police believe that...' or, 'The police were suspicious that ...' Those are tricky areas you should check out with a libel lawyer. In fact, any time you write a true crime book, you should submit your manuscript for vetting by a libel lawyer. Your publisher will do that for you; they don't want to get sued either."

The Future of True Crime

True crime is undergoing major changes right now, Carol Soret Cope believes. "There are only a handful of people who can sell a true crime book these days. Ann Rule, Joe McGinniss, for example. The problem is that the big stories—O.J. Simpson, Susan Smith, the Menendez brothers—go immediately to the tabloids and TV movies, and there's always a bunch of competing books. I'm not going to spend my time being the eighty-fifth person to write a book about O.J. Simpson.

"What I see happening in the true crime market is that it's becoming much more regional. There'll always be a handful of major stories, but they get pretty much milked. Unless you have backing from a big publisher to pay you to follow one of the big cases, it's better to find a story closer to home. Concentrate on stories that have the usual elements—intrigue, sex, murder, and maybe a macabre element to it, such as with Jeffrey Dahmer.

"What interests me is the upstanding citizen who is leading a double life. And I think people are always interested in the fall of the mighty. Someone who seems to have it all—then you see the dark side of him.

"There'll always be a steady market for true crime, but I think publishers are going to look more and more to the regional stories, push them regionally, sell them regionally, and leave the big stories to the established writers."

Carol Soret Cope has another book in the works, this time a techno-thriller. She still practices law in Miami.

Mystery Writers of America

Mystery writers of America (MWA), founded in 1945, is a professional writers' association dedicated to mystery, crime, and suspense writing. Past presidents include Sue Grafton, Elmore Leonard, Mary Higgins Clark, Gregory McDonald, Phyllis Whitney, and Raymond Chandler.

There are three categories of membership:

ACTIVE MEMBERS These are published professional writers of fiction or nonfiction in the mystery, crime, or suspense field. Only active members may vote or hold office.

ASSOCIATE MEMBERS These are professionals in allied fields: editors, publishers, writers in other fields, reporters, critics, agents, publicists, librarians, booksellers, law enforcement personnel, private investigators, and other professionals involved in activities related to writing mystery, crime, and suspense.

AFFILIATE MEMBERS These are people who have demonstrated the ability to write a full-length novel or a short story. They must have a completed manuscript—and a rejection slip. An acceptance letter would put the writer in the Active Member category. The rejection slip shows that the member has written a book or story and has submitted it for publication. Fans of mystery books are not included in this category, unless they are also writers.

The national office is located in New York, and at this writing, there are nine chapters located in the following areas: Boston, Chicago, San Francisco, Los Angeles, Denver, Houston, Seattle, and the state of Florida, headquartered in Fort Lauderdale. In addition to the national office, New York also has its own local chapter.

Membership fees are paid annually to the national office and cover membership in a local chapter. To find the address of the local chapter nearest you, contact the national office, whose address is listed in the appendix.

The national office, besides keeping all the local chapters together, is basically a watchdog of legislation and tax situations that affect writers. They are allied with the Authors Guild and other similar professional organizations. At the heart of the organization is the interest of the professional writer. The national office will handle any grievances a member might have, such as a problem with a contract. This is a free service to members.

The national office maintains an extensive library of reference books and critical studies in the mystery, crime, and suspense fields. Some of MWA's members are well known people in criminology and crime investigation, and if a member needs source material, a phone call to "national" will point him or her in the right direction.

In addition, MWA puts out an anthology every few years, a collection of the work of esteemed members.

MWA awards the Edgar Allan Poe Award for excellence in mystery, crime, and suspense writing. They also offer the Grand Master Award for lifetime achievement in mystery, crime, and suspense writing. The first recipient was Agatha Christie; other recipients have included Mickey Spillane, Lawrence Block, Tony Hillerman, and John D. MacDonald.

A Look at a Local MWA Chapter

Dianne Ell served as president of the Florida chapter of MWA from 1993 to 1995. She is still active in the membership.

"We try to establish a forum here in the state of Florida where professional writers, people in allied fields, and those who want to be published can meet and work together.

"One way we accomplish this is through monthly meetings. Generally we have a guest speaker, someone who is a professional in the crime or criminal investigation field. This is to keep people abreast of changes and cases going on that might be of interest to them as writers.

"We also do full-day writer workshops on mystery, crime, and suspense writing; on writing the short story; and on writing the screenplay. These are held intermittently, every six months or so.

"We participate in book fairs. This gives our published authors an opportunity to have their work exposed to the public.

"We also publish a newsletter, *The Die-Gest*, and this is sent to members, libraries, bookstores, and other MWA chapters throughout the country. In the newsletter we include information on what's happening currently in the publishing field, anything that would be of interest. General fiction, legislation, electronic rights. We also focus on what's happening in the state, and we profile our members so they know who everyone is.

"Then there's our biggie—SleuthFest. This is our major annual mystery, crime, and suspense writers' conference. It's a three-day event with lectures on various aspects of writing both mystery and general fiction. Speakers are generally MWA members, particularly Florida chapter members. This is a way to help them promote their books. We have quite a list of well-known writers: Edna Buchanan, Dick Francis, Elmore Leonard, Barbara Parket, David Kaufelt, to name just a few.

"This conference isn't just for members or budding writers. Many of the general public who are not writers but are interested in mysteries have been attending. We cover all different topics and have author panels, and we also bring in editors and agents from New York. They spend three days with us, and we set up appointments and give attendees a chance to pitch their books to them. It's a great way to get personal feedback.

"Other local chapters have different events: northern California holds Mystery Week, for example, and in Chicago they put on a one-day event called Dark and Stormy Nights. The best way to find out what's happening in your area is to contact the national office of MWA."

Sisters in Crime

Sisters in Crime was organized in 1986 by some women mystery writers who were aware of that fact that although women were writing half of the mysteries in the country, they were getting only about 10 percent of the reviews. The purpose of Sisters in Crime is to create a level playing field for women who write mysteries.

"Actually, men are also members of Sisters in Crime; we've got some very good 'brothers in crime,'" says Patricia Sprinkle, publicity chairperson for this national organization. "We're open to both men and women who happen to feel that women writers should be getting a fair shake.

"We're a very supportive organization for writers. We meet twice a year in conjunction with other mystery conferences. We have an open meeting at Bouchercon, which takes place every October in different locales. That's the big national conference. Bookstores, writers, and fans in different cities sponsor it each year. In 1994 it was held in Seattle; in 1995, in Nottingham, England; in 1996, in Minneapolis.

"The other meeting is called Malice Domestic. This conference is held every April in Bethesda, Maryland, for people who write traditional mysteries. Sisters in Crime is open to women who write hard-boiled and soft-boiled, who write PI, who write amateur sleuth, and police procedurals. Some write suspense mysteries. But Malice Domestic is specifically for writers and readers of the traditional mystery. The traditional mystery usually has an amateur sleuth. It takes place in a small family or village setting with a small circle of people. The clues are all there so the reader can solve it. There's very little violence. There could be a romantic interest, but not heavy on the sex. They used to be all written by dead English women, but now there are a lot of women, including me, who write that type of book.

"We also put out a newsletter four times a year. Members can vote at the meetings. We have some local chapters, but you don't have to be in a local chapter. The main benefit of membership is that we know other people. It's a networking organization. We have a speakers' bureau and put together panels of writers to speak in bookstores. For libraries we put out our own *Books in Print*, which comes out twice a year, and a directory of all our members' names and addresses. We have 2800 members. Not all are writers. Some are readers; some are bookstores or libraries.

"A lot of our members are 'wannabe' writers. As we point out, all of us started out as wannabe writers. But we don't exist to help wannabe writers get published. I think each of us works with wannabe writers to help them out, but that's not our purpose. We do introduce beginners to agents and editors at conferences and give advice, but we aren't responsible for making submissions or arranging for agents to take a writer on.

"Members travel together, do panels together, help each other set up book signings. We have a fairly extensive list of bookstores and managers so we can keep track of who's who. We monitor reviews for one another. Basically we provide a lot of support for each other."

For more information contact the national office of Sisters in Crime in Lawrence, Kansas. Their address is listed in the appendix.

Further Reading

No writer's desk is complete without a good stock of the right reference books. Writer's Digest Books, an imprint of F&W Publications, has the most extensive list of how-to books for writers.

Here is just a sampling, taken from *The Howdunit Writing Series* from Writer's Digest's catalog.

Newton, Michael. *Armed and Dangerous: A Writer's Guide to Weapons.*

Wingate, Anne. *Scene of the Crime: A Writer's Guide to Crime Scene Investigation.*

Blythe, Hal, Charlie Sweet, and John Handreth. *Private Eyes: A Writer's Guide to Private Investigators.*

Stevens, Serita Deborah. *Deadly Doses: A Writer's Guide to Poisons.*

Wilson, Keith D. *Cause of Death: A Writer's Guide to Death, Murder & Forensic Medicine.*

Bintliff, Russell. *Police Procedural: A Writer's Guide to the Police and How They Work.*

Norville, Barbara. *Writing the Modern Mystery.*

Grafton, Sue, ed. *Writing Mysteries: A Handbook by the Mystery Writers of America.*

Collingwood, Donna, ed. *Mystery Writer's Market Place and Sourcebook.* Part market guide, part resource guide, and part forum, this directory is an indispensable writing and marketing companion for mystery, suspense, and crime writers.

All Writer's Digest books may be ordered through your local bookstore or by contacting the publishers directly at:

Writer's Digest Books
1507 Dana Avenue
Cincinnati, OH 45207
(800) 289-0963

CHAPTER THREE

A Nose for News

Investigative Reporters

D o you have a nose for news? Are you up on current events, aware of how your government operates? Would you enjoy sleuthing and snooping, uncovering scams and fraudulent practices, or breaking stories that will affect the lives of your readers? If so, then a career as an investigative reporter might be the right path for you to take.

Settings for Investigative Reporters

People want to know what's going on around them. Just look at the popularity of TV magazine shows; *60 Minutes, 20/20,* and *48 Hours* are just three of a full lineup on the various networks. "Tabloid" shows are also popular. *Current Edition* and *Hard Copy* seem never to lack for ratings. TV news programs, from local to national, also abound. CNN, for example, runs news spots all day long.

All the different kinds of TV news and magazine programs utilize the services of investigative reporters. Newspapers and magazines do as well.

In this chapter you will meet two investigative reporters: one works for a major television station, the other for a large-circulation newspaper. Listen and you will learn what their jobs really entail, how they got started, and how you might.

Working on Television: Al Sunshine

Al Sunshine is a familiar face all through south Florida. He is perhaps best known for his Shame on You reports seen on WCIX, the CBS affiliate in Miami.

"Shame on You is an investigative consumer action franchise for the station," Al explains. "We basically look at government incompetence, pollution, unscrupulous business practices, and we try to personalize the stories for people who are involved. After a lot of investigation and a lot of careful writing and production, we let people literally shake their fingers and say, 'Shame on You,' to the bad guys."

Al Sunshine is in the middle of an impressive career that began as early as his high school days in the metropolitan New York–New Jersey area.

"As far back as high school, I had a great curiosity about what was going on about me, and I started writing and taking pictures for the high school paper. I was curious not only about the events that were happening, but I wanted to look deeper, to get under the surface and to find out why they were happening. Why some systems that were there to protect us weren't working, perhaps.

"From high school I went to the University of Miami. That was in 1968. I started off in marine biology, from there went to psychology, and from there into mass communications. I bounced around, like so many kids did. I graduated in 1972 with a major in psychology and communications.

"The interesting thing for me during that time, in '68, '69, and '70, was that it was during the era of confrontation and a lot of questions and campus activism. There was Watergate and Kent State. I literally went from being a student at the University of Miami, working for the university newspaper covering campus politics and campus news, to Watergate, Kent State, and tear gas at the Democratic and Republican conventions in '72. I cut my teeth working television on some very important issues.

"Miami back in the sixties and seventies had a fantastic national reputation. We got involved in a lot of stories—anti-Castro militants, drug dealers, refugees, political intrigue. A lot of other prominent investigative reporters have come out of Miami. Brian Ross worked in Miami for quite a long time; John Scott of *Dateline* was based here. Today Miami still has a national reputation for investigative journalism.

"I started working with WTVJ, which was the CBS affiliate at the time, and for twelve or thirteen years I covered a lot of great stories. Then I went to work for CNN in about 1983. I covered the space shuttle, and *Challenger*, and space program problems at NASA. I also got involved covering the Contras behind enemy lines for CNN in Nicaragua. I was also covering the covert airline supply operation for the Contras that was based out of south Florida.

"I went back to work for CBS in 1989 and got volunteered for the Shame on You spot. I've also been on *Geraldo* three or four times, covering some national stories. We did scams against women— diet and health fraud, stories on modeling agency scams, and the dark side of the modeling industry, those that scam young girls into paying thousands of dollars with the promise of a career that never materializes.

"I was also on *Geraldo* with an investigation I'd done into unsanitary school cafeterias. That investigation was shown in the Florida legislature and, I'm proud to say, resulted in new disclosure laws requiring schools to post their health inspections.

"Our investigations have been shown extensively throughout the state, and I've been asked to testify in some state committees. I've frankly lost track of how many laws we've gotten on the books as a result of our stories.

"I think the stories that have had the most impact have been those on car repair fraud and scams. We showed frustrations of consumers who were ripped off by unscrupulous mechanics. Not only do we have car repair regulations in Dade and Broward counties as a result of our stories, but we now have a statewide car repair protection law for consumers.

"The story that most affected me personally was something that happened twenty years ago: two kids who were abducted at gunpoint from a church ice cream social. We heard about it Monday morning, and about an hour after that, we got reports that two bodies had been found. As I was interviewing the police, a stranger next to me collapsed in tears. His son had been missing, and when he heard that the police were at a crime scene, he hurried over to find out what was happening. As it turned out, his son was one of the victims.

"It was absolutely a gut-wrenching occurrence to have someone listening in on the interview and then collapse when he realized it had been his son who'd been murdered.

"I cite this as an example, that this is not a career that you are going to be working nine-to-five and walking away from. You'll be dancing in and out of other people's tragedies, and it will take a toll on you. It absolutely will."

Some Advice from Al Sunshine

"You cannot take no for an answer from either a prospective employer or someone you're trying to talk to as a source on a story. It's the kind of work that no one is going to help you with. It's something you have to have burning inside you, an incredible desire to want to do this in the light of a lot of adversity.

"It's much more than a job; it's almost a lifestyle. You need the ability to keep your eyes and ears open for possible stories and the ability to hear a lot of people's tragedies and put them into perspective. You have to try to make a positive change come from it all.

"I think there's a responsibility with journalists that is more and more being recognized. You can't simply walk away from a story after just showing the problem. You also have to show the other side and give your viewers or readers a perspective on why things are happening. You have to offer a possible answer and a possible way of trying to prevent future problems.

"Journalism for the most part is very good at tearing down institutions and tearing down politicians. But in all fairness you owe your viewers and readers some answers.

"How should you prepare yourself? Within the news business it's very controversial whether you should study journalism or whether you should get an all-around education in liberal arts. That's something everybody has to decide for themselves, but I'd caution you that the world out there does not revolve around journalism. It revolves around families, work, education, history. You can't be a good reporter unless you can write a good sentence, unless you understand economics, unless you understand local government. A liberal arts education will help you to become a well-rounded individual."

Working for a Newspaper: Nancy McVicar

Nancy McVicar is a senior writer at the *Sun-Sentinel*, a newspaper in Fort Lauderdale, Florida, with a circulation of about one million.

She works for the "Lifestyle" section, which has a health page every Thursday. Her stories also appear in other sections: recently a package of stories on the resurgence of infectious diseases began on the front cover.

Her articles focus on health, medicine, and fitness. Her work has been nominated for the Pulitzer Prize seven times, and several of her stories have won national awards.

Nancy talks about her job:

"One aspect of medical writing is investigative. You may have to start from scratch, search documents, knock on doors. One investigative story I did here was on HMOs and how they treat their Medicare-age patients. People over sixty-five on Medicare have the option of joining an HMO, which is supposed to provide them with all the care they would get under Medicare but for less money. As a writer I was getting all sorts of complaints from people saying things like, 'They let my husband die; they didn't send him to the specialist they should have.' There's money involved. The more care you give, the less money goes into the HMO's pocket, so there's a financial disincentive to give care. Two other people, cowriters and investigators, and I spent six months on an investigation. You can do it by yourself, but it goes much faster if you have help. You may have to sift through tons of documents, which we did. We concluded that there were a lot of problems. Once we brought them to light, the federal government promised that they would fix them. They worked on it, but they haven't fixed anything yet. So my coworkers did another story, a follow-up, which brought more problems to light. And again the government is promising to make changes to protect people's lives.

"It was a five-day series that went out over the wire services and got a lot of exposure. It also won a long list of awards for the three of us. It's gratifying to be a change agent: that's the whole point of an investigative piece, to get some change going."

Nancy was the first to break the story "Are Your Cellular Telephones Safe?" She produced two or three articles on the topic. The stories went out over the wire and also ended up on *20/20* and *60 Minutes*. The General Accounting Office, the investigative arm of the U.S. Congress, was asked to do an in-depth report on whether cellular phones are safe, based on the stories Nancy wrote. The report has not yet been presented, but it's due out soon.

Nancy explains how she got involved:

"I was doing a bigger piece on brain tumors and the latest treatment. In the course of doing this, I kept hearing that some people were saying that their cellular phones had given them their brain tumors. My first reaction was, 'Yeah, right,' but then when I started investigating, I found out it could be true. There's no proof that it is, but even the phone companies have started putting disclaimers in their manuals saying, Don't hold this thing close to your head."

Nancy also did a piece on emergency rooms and how they are being used in place of the doctor's office for people who don't have insurance. "The point was that professionals who are trained to handle trauma are instead handling sore throats and sniffles. It was a mini-investigation. I spent time at two different hospitals observing what went on during the day and did a whole-page article with pictures that won a national award with a cash prize.

"There's so much out there to write about," Nancy says, "that you can really pick and choose what you're interested in or what you think your readers will be interested in. It's not like next week I'm going to be writing the same old story about some council meeting.

"And there is a wealth of experts to talk to who are willing to give you their time. But you have to know enough to be able to ask the right questions. You have to background yourself a bit before you get a doctor on the phone. You want to be able to ask intelligent questions and not waste his time.

"It's more than just medical writing because I've also been doing some stories on health care reform, which is another whole issue, and that's taken up my time over the last couple of years. I try to explain the plan to readers so they can understand it, using actual people and their circumstances to tell the story. I look at questions such as why we need health care reform and what it means to the average person.

"Another story I recently did was about how antibiotics are losing their effectiveness because we're overusing them. I wouldn't call it breaking news; it's more a trend story. Here's something I think we need to be worried about, and why.

"In researching my stories, I use a number of avenues. We have an electronic database so I can ask our resource center here to do a search on what's been written in other publications about a particular subject.

"We can also get on the 'information superhighway,' Internet, and make queries about things. I was preparing to do an interview with Kristine Gebbie, the 'AIDS czar' appointed by Clinton, so I put out a question on the Internet asking people in the AIDS community what they would like to know from this woman. I got some really good suggestions for the interview.

"As it turned out, between the time I set it up and the time I actually did the interview, she resigned. It made an even better story about why she was quitting.

"For other sources I talk to doctors and others in the medical community, and I read a lot, particularly medical journals. I subscribe to the *Journal of the American Medical Association* and *The New England Journal of Medicine*, and I get probably half a dozen medical newsletters, from Johns Hopkins to the Mayo Clinic or the Lahey Clinic in Massachusetts. I also receive more consumer-oriented publications. Consumer Reports puts out a health letter, and the Center for Science in the Public Interest has a couple of publications, including one on nutrition. They're the ones who broke the story on movie theater popcorn and how full of fat it is.

"I also get a lot of phone calls from interested readers who say, 'I wonder if you know anything about such and such,' or, 'I read there's a new treatment for high blood pressure, and what can you tell me about it?' If I get enough calls on a particular subject, I might decide there's an interest here that needs to be addressed and start researching it and do a story about it.

"Every once in a while I do a question-and-answer column, when I think it's called for. Recently there was a case of hantavirus in Dade County. There had been an outbreak of it in the Southwest last year, and it killed about half the people who got it. It's a deadly virus, and it turned up in south Dade County. I did a Q&A to let readers know they didn't have to be too concerned, that it's not really contagious. You get it from breathing the dried-up urine of rodents that are infected.

"Finding ideas for stories is not my problem; finding time to do all the stories is the bigger problem. You can't do them in one afternoon. You have to use multiple sources. You have to call at least two or three experts, even though you might not end up quoting them all in the story. But you can never do a one-source medical story.

"We don't have a quota for the number of stories we're going to write. We don't do breaking stories that much. I'll take a whole list of stories to my editor, and we discuss them and decide which we should do first. We work with the photo people and our graphic staff so we can illustrate them."

Getting Started as a Health and Medical Writer

"I sort of fell into it," Nancy McVicar says. "I had done almost everything else on a newspaper, and when this job was offered, it sounded appealing. But a lot of people go into journalism initially and know they want to be medical writers. They can then pick their courses in school to get a good background.

"Take some combination of journalism and science and medicine courses. There are even some people who have gone to medical school. I think the *New York Times* has a medical writer who is an M.D., and ABC has Dr. Timothy Johnson.

"Salaries will vary. Small papers don't pay very much at all, and large papers can pay very well. If you're just starting, you could find yourself in the low- to mid-twenties range or less. But many small papers don't even necessarily have health and medical writers; they rely on the wire services to provide them with stories.

"With a few years' experience under your belt, you can move up the pay ladder to thirty or forty thousand; with several years at a large newspaper, your salary could even be in the fifty thousand range.

"But most of the time, before you could be hired at a large newspaper, you'd have to have experience at a smaller one. You can start off doing general assignments before you move on to your plum position somewhere else."

Nancy McVicar's Background

Nancy always knew she wanted to be a writer, but she started out writing novels and poetry. "I still do that," Nancy says, "but not very much. You have to be able to make a living, and you can do that as an investigative reporter.

"I don't really have a medical background as such, but I do have a lot of medical people in my family, and at one point I did entertain the thought of going into some kind of medical field myself. I've always had an interest in it and I think it helps."

Nancy's first job came about as a result of a blind ad she answered for "someone with a good English background." The job turned out to be for an assistant to the society editor at a small paper in Kansas. She started out writing weddings and engagements and then branched out, doing features on her own that were then published.

"I also was an editor for seven years," Nancy says. "I did enjoy it, but I chose to go back to writing because it's what I prefer. It's a lifestyle choice for me. I'd rather do the sleuthing that it takes to produce a story than deal with the nuts and bolts of going to meetings every day and editing other people's work. I prefer the writing; it's more creative.

"And with health writing, the job is never boring. Medicine is always changing; there's always something new."

CHAPTER FOUR

The World of Crime

C rime doesn't pay, they say, but that old saw is aimed at criminals. On the other side of the law, there is a vast array of careers—and they all offer legitimate paychecks.

But there's no room for armchair mystery buffs here. Any of the following careers will have you out where the action is. Some of the work is frustrating, some of it involves danger, but there's no greater reward than tracking down real criminals, prosecuting them, and seeing justice at work.

Have a look at the following list of career paths from which you can choose. Then read on to see what they involve.

Law enforcement
    Police detectives
    Special agents
      FBI
      Customs
      ATF
      Secret Service
      IRS
      DEA
    Arson investigators

Attorneys at law
    For the defense
    For the prosecution

Private investigation
Undercover work
Insurance fraud
Art forgery

Law Enforcement

The safety of our nation's cities, towns, and highways greatly depends on the work of police officers, deputy sheriffs, detectives, and special agents, whose responsibilities range from controlling traffic to preventing and investigating crimes.

As civilian police department employees and private security personnel increasingly assume routine police duties, police and detectives are able to spend more time fighting serious crime.

POLICE OFFICERS AND DETECTIVES who work in small communities and rural areas have many duties. In the course of a day's work, they may direct traffic at the scene of a fire, investigate a burglary, or give first aid to an accident victim. In a large police department, by contrast, officers usually are assigned to a specific type of duty. Most officers are detailed either to patrol or to traffic duty; smaller numbers are assigned to special work, such as accident prevention. Others are experts in chemical and microscopic analysis, firearms identification, and handwriting and fingerprint identification. In very large cities officers may be assigned to special task forces, such as homicide, burglary, and even SWAT teams.

DETECTIVES AND SPECIAL AGENTS are plainclothes investigators who gather facts and collect evidence for criminal cases. They conduct interviews, examine records, observe the activities of suspects, and participate in raids or arrests.

FEDERAL BUREAU OF INVESTIGATION (FBI) AGENTS investigate violations of federal laws in connection with bank robberies, theft of government property, organized crime, espionage, sabotage, kidnapping, and terrorism. Agents with specialized training usually work on cases related to their background. For example, agents with an accounting background may investigate white-collar crimes such as bank embezzlements or fraudulent bankruptcies and land deals. Frequently agents must testify in court about cases that they investigate.

The U.S. Department of the Treasury employs special agents who work for the U.S. Customs Service; the Bureau of Alcohol, Tobacco, and Firearms; the U.S. Secret Service; and the Internal Revenue Service.

CUSTOMS AGENTS   enforce laws to prevent the smuggling of goods across U.S. borders.

ALCOHOL, TOBACCO, AND FIREARMS (ATF) AGENTS   might investigate suspected illegal sales of guns or the underpayment of taxes by a liquor or cigarette manufacturer.

U.S. SECRET SERVICE AGENTS   protect the president and vice president and their immediate families, and also presidential candidates, ex-presidents, and foreign dignitaries visiting the United States. In addition, Secret Service agents investigate counterfeiting, the forgery of government checks or bonds, and the fraudulent use of credit cards.

INTERNAL REVENUE SERVICE SPECIAL AGENTS   collect evidence against individuals and companies that are evading the payment of federal taxes.

DRUG ENFORCEMENT ADMINISTRATION (DEA) AGENTS   conduct criminal investigations of illicit drug activity. They compile evidence and arrest individuals who violate federal drug laws. They may prepare reports that are used in criminal proceedings, give testimony in court, or develop evidence that justifies the seizure of financial assets gained from illegal activity.

ARSON INVESTIGATORS   generally work for fire departments but they cooperate with local police departments and often testify in court. They start out as fully trained firefighters before moving into an investigator's role.

Ramesh Nyberg, Homicide Detective

Ramesh Nyberg is a homicide detective with the Metro-Dade Police Department in Miami, Florida. He started his career in 1979.

Ramesh talks about his work:

"I don't think there's any greater weapon in a policeman's arsenal than his own ears and his ability to listen. In street police work, when you're a uniformed police officer, you have to be very aware of what people are doing and saying. You can't take a report from someone without listening to them. For purposes of your own safety, you have to listen carefully to what they're saying, their tone of voice, whether it's rising or falling. I think young police officers miss this a lot, but there are things people say and things they won't say that they'll only hint at, whether consciously or subconsciously. They have the potential to tell you a lot of things, but without your asking the proper questions, they won't say anything.

"This becomes even more important in detective work. Our interviews in Homicide are very thorough. One thing we do in Homicide that people don't see on television very often is that while some detectives are working inside the house or the crime scene, there will be other detectives knocking on every door on that block and possibly the next block. Very often people will see things, hear things, or know things but won't say a word until someone knocks on their door. Maybe a week later we'll try a block a little further away that we hadn't tried earlier, and we'll knock on people's doors there. And a little old lady will be in there and say, 'Oh, I heard a gunshot and saw a black car leaving.' We ask her why she didn't tell anybody. Her answer: 'Nobody asked me.' That's very common, and very often, too, the murderer might live in the neighborhood, or the murderer might already be known and somebody next door might know something about it. 'Yeah, I remember last week him talking about killin' his wife. He's been complaining about her all week.' That type of thing.

"Here's something else that's important that you don't see in the movies or on television. When you make an arrest, the case is only beginning. On TV after the arrest, it's over. You get the closing credits while everyone is slapping each other on the back and going out for a beer. That's not the way it happens in police work. Very often when an arrest is made, a whole new avenue of the case opens up.

"If you're working a case where you have an unknown offender, you've got a dead body and that's it. The first thing you do is start with the victim. You try to find out who the victim's friends, enemies, lovers, relatives, coworkers were—everything about the victim you possibly can. You're looking for reasons why this person is dead and who would have the best opportunity, means, and motive to kill him.

"But you can't even begin guessing about motive until you know where the victim's haunts are and who he or she doesn't trust, and so on.

"Once you start working that whole circle around the victim, and let's say you develop a suspect, and you sit down with that person and he confesses. Or for whatever reasons you're able to identify the killer. Once you've made that identification, you then have another whole circle to investigate—his or her family, friends, coworkers, etc. You might have to get search warrants for his car, for his house. 'Oh, he took a trip to Boston a week after the homicide? Let's see who he visited there.' What he might have told that person. 'Oh, an ex-girlfriend? Let's go talk to her.' You can't in good conscience omit that. There's only a small chance he told her anything, but you have to follow the lead. I've had to travel a lot in the course of my work. I've even been to other countries—Jamaica, Costa Rica, Canada. Miami is such a transient area. Our department is probably much more generous with travel budgets than others.

"What you want to do in a homicide case is get as much evidence against the suspect as possible. These cases are so heavily scrutinized—if you watched one-tenth of the O.J. Simpson trial, well, that's typical of a homicide case. The defense tries to discredit everything and everybody that the state puts up. You've got to have overkill, you've got to have more than enough evidence in a homicide case. If you get two or three people who say, 'Oh yeah, I saw him do it,' well, you still have to look for four or five other witnesses who can say the same thing.

"You might have enough to make an arrest, but to convict you have to continue to try to get more."

Metro-Dade's Cold Case Squad

Ramesh Nyberg is currently on the cold case squad handling old, unsolved murders.

"Cold cases or active investigations—they each have their advantages. There's a real thrill to getting a fresh case and going out and working it, developing leads and seeing it progress. You can't really match that thrill. But it's also very hard on the family life. You're doing it all the time, you're always getting called out, and it's very taxing.

"With cold cases you're on a different schedule. You can work until five, then go home and have a more stable lifestyle. For my purposes I prefer this assignment now.

"We have five detectives and a sergeant on our squad, and we're actively working ten to fifteen cases. There are over a thousand waiting, but our success rate is not bad at all. Since 1982 or '83, I think we've closed 120 cases. Since I've been on the squad we've closed quite a few. It's a good feeling to go back and work a case that, for whatever reasons, wasn't solved earlier. And it's not that the detectives assigned to the original case didn't do a good job. It's always a question of time. When you're dealing with active cases, there's always another case given to you to juggle. We don't have to do that. We're not interrupted. When we make an appointment with a witness, we're able to keep it. We have the luxury of time to work on the case.

"I enjoy the ongoing challenge of trying to track down homicides. Homicide is the worst crime there is, and I like the fact we can work on cases that have no statute of limitations. That old cliche 'getting away with murder' is not really true.

"I don't envy robbery detectives. They work very hard, but often it's for naught. They're able to find the offenders, but often nothing happens to them in the court system. Robbers are getting these ridiculously light sentences. It's not until they actually kill someone that they get any real time."

The Stresses of Police Work

"I think the criminal justice system is one of the biggest generators of stress in our work. Having to deal with a system that has been created and manipulated by attorneys is a very difficult system to deal with. And here's one of the great myths that Hollywood has created, that there's this big, cooperative effort between police, court, and prosecutors, that it's all one big engine that's geared toward putting people in prison. But it's not like that at all. The prosecutors have their own agenda, and it's not our agenda at all. Their agenda is to move cases and to try cases that are only winnable. Our agenda is to get these people off the street. They don't want marginal cases. And there are times you can't do that. There are times when we have enough probable cause to arrest someone. He's a hazard and we need to get him off the street. Prosecuting him might be difficult, we might lose, but let's go for it. We might win. You're constantly arguing your position, and that creates stress. The justice system in general is just not a pro-law-enforcement system.

"Then there's the bureaucratic nature of police departments. The way we work is not one you'd find in a modern successful, growing corporation that is constantly striving for excellence. And I don't mean this to demean the department; it's an excellent one.

But it's the nature of the infrastructure of police work. We have, for example, a department that has a lot of money. But sometimes the money is spent on things that are not directly applied to bettering investigations. I think you should look at what the most important investigations are—sexual batteries, homicides, robberies—and give those people the best equipment and resources so they can do their work. Instead the money goes to bigger cars for the chiefs, cellular phones to put in those cars. The detectives don't get enough phones or cars, and so we see some of the money being wasted. And you see the department much more concerned with presenting some sort of veiled public image rather than really doing the best possible work we can.

"The actual physical part of seeing bodies shot up and cut up or whatever is something you learn how to handle pretty fast. You get over that initial shock after seeing it three or four times. It becomes pretty routine. A bludgeoned or dismembered body becomes nothing more than another piece of evidence. We learn how to go into a certain mode when we're at a crime scene to look at these things objectively and without emotion. But I think it does affect us. You can't totally disregard the natural human feeling of being revolted or infuriated by a lot of things you see.

"I think this particularly happens when it comes to innocent victims. But we don't see a lot of innocent victims. A lot of people we deal with put themselves in bad positions. The majority of our victims are drug dealers, robbers, swindlers: people who are out there committing crimes themselves. What you hear on the news—the child accidentally shot in a drive-by, the tourist stabbed, the suburban housewife murdered—that actually represents only a small fragment of our victims.

"These are widely publicized because they're shocking stories, and people can relate to these victims. But the news doesn't tend to report the onslaught of cases we get where one crack dealer kills another or a smuggler dies shot, bound, and gagged in the trunk of a car. They don't hold the same emotional level that other cases do.

"Cases involving children affect people a lot, and we're no different that way. We're no more able to shrug that off than any other average person. Some of us might fool ourselves into thinking we can, but we can't.

"We have a child exploitation unit, but I don't think I could work that. I happen to have a very sensitive spot with children. I would not be able to handle that emotionally for very long.

"There's not nearly as much danger as you see on television. Homicide detectives don't get into running gun battles as often as they do on television shows. It's really a pretty safe job. When we get to a crime scene, the crime is over. There are uniformed officers standing over it; the scene has been roped off and secured.

"Going to interview a suspect, however, could be dangerous. If we know the person we're going to interview is a suspect, depending on the level of contact we're going to have with him, we'll govern ourselves accordingly. We'll say, 'This guy probably did it; he looks like a good candidate.' Then we'll take two detectives, maybe three, to make our first contact, to feel him out and to see what he says or how he reacts. If it's someone we're planning to arrest, that's a different story. We'll go in with more people. On rare occasions we might get surprised by someone who we didn't think of as a suspect. We go to interview a neighbor, for example, who turns out to be the offender.

"That's why we always are on our guard and we never work alone. There's a lot more interaction going on about decisions that have to be made, with meetings between the detectives and between the detectives and the prosecutors, than you see on television. We do everything strategically. We are always trying to anticipate what we're going to face in court, and we try to decide ahead of time what the right strategies are we'll follow. That TV image of the lone cop going off on his own is pure fantsy. You don't have detectives working a homicide by themselves. I love Columbo and how at the end he always describes his train of thought and what led him to the suspect. But it just doesn't work that way.

"As far as corruption I can speak for myself and the rest of my squad. We don't have any time for corruption. I think I'd give that about half a second. I think you make your decision—you're either going to be a crook or a cop. Don't try to be both. I'd probably have less contempt for someone who's just an all-out crook than somebody who is a police officer and wants to be a crook at the same time. That person I could really hate.

"Another part of police work you don't see is the constant joking and camaraderie. I don't think you could survive without it. The work is so intensely serious, and the topics we deal with are so grim sometimes, so if you're constantly taking it to heart you'd have a lot of tension in the workplace. We're constantly finding ways to break the tension."

How Ramesh Got Started

"It was not one of these things that I always wanted to be a policeman as a kid. I remember that I wanted to be a bus driver. I didn't really gain a keen interest in it until I was about eighteen. I was attending Miami-Dade Community College, and I used to study with a friend who listened to a police scanner. It fascinated me, and I decided to sign up for an observer ride. When I was out there with them and saw what the police did firsthand, how they utilized all their senses—not just their authority, but their intellect, too—it really interested me a lot. Two or three observer rides later, I was pretty much hooked on the idea of police work as a profession.

"Through word of mouth and through the paper, I learned which departments were hiring and I started putting in my applications. My first receptive response was from Opalocka, and that's where I started out. They sent me to the police academy, which at the time was held at the north campus of Miami-Dade Community College. It's called the Southeast Florida Institute of Criminal Justice. At that time the program was five and a half months. Now I think it's up to eight months.

"I stayed at Opalocka for one year; then I moved to the North Miami Police Department and was there for two years, from 1980 to

1982. But I was getting tired of small police departments. Opalocka was a thirty-three–officer department; North Miami had about ninety. The opportunities to move around and do different kinds of police work, such as detective work, were much more scarce.

"With the county there are any number of detective bureaus to move around in. It's a police force of 3000 plus. There are many more options. In 1982 I was able to transfer to Metro-Dade. I had to stay on patrol for almost three years, going out on a range of calls, covering the beat. In 1985 I was made a detective."

Do You Have What It Takes?

"This job requires that you have a certain personality," Ramesh Nyberg explains. "You have to be flexible, tenacious, and have convictions. If you don't, then what are you doing there?

"There are times in homicide when you almost have to forget you're a cop. If you're sitting down with someone and conducting an intimate interview, you cannot let your authority get in your way. You can't get offended or react the way a typical young cop on the street would react. If someone calls you a pig, for example, you can't have a macho response. And I mean that to apply to both men and women.

"It's a thing about the badge. If you get insulted on the street, you can't back down because you'll be perceived as weak. And people will try to take advantage of you. In the interview room you have to be more on their level to be effective. You have to get them to trust you. To do that you have to be able to put your emotion aside.

"Police work really involves just hard work and determination, observation, and common sense. I think that when people watch television shows about police work, they see cops as beings with some sort of special powers. And I think people who want to become police officers and do become police officers are special people in many ways, but it's simply a matter of applying yourself and being objective. You can't get too locked into one train of thought.

"If you enter this profession, don't expect to change too much. A lot of cops think they're going to be able to change people. You might affect a couple of people's lives, but basically we're not going to change crime, we're not going to stop drugs. I don't think it's a fatalistic attitude; I think it's just reality. On the bright side, we're always going to have a job.

"This is my career and I love my career, but it's not my life. I think you should have other interests to keep yourself on an even keel."

Ramesh Nyberg has followed his own advice. He makes time in his busy schedule to work at freelance writing and has sold numerous articles to magazines, including "The Ten Most Common Crime Writing Mistakes," to *Writer's Digest* magazine.

He has just finished his novel and is in the process of submitting it to an agent.

Undercover Cops

Whereas homicide detectives almost never work undercover, there are many other units that utilize clandestine means to accomplish their goal—catching the bad guys. Detective Sergeant Timothy Bronson has been with the Fort Lauderdale Police Department in Florida since 1981. For many of those years, he worked undercover in specialized tactical units. He also worked on the SWAT team.

"I was a great reader of mysteries when I was a kid; anything to do with serial killers, rapists, that sort of thing. And I think that's how the seed got planted.

"I got a job as a security guard in California and I was on the list to take the LAPD test, but then all of a sudden there was a hiring freeze. My father called to tell me that my hometown, Little Falls, New York, was giving the test. That was in 1977. I started as a patrolman, but I wanted to work for a bigger police department. In 1981 I started looking around. I got hired in Palm Beach County and in Baltimore; then, Fort Lauderdale.

"When I started in Fort Lauderdale, I worked the midnight shift for a year and a half, then went into the tactical unit, which is a plainclothes undercover unit. We tried to get robberies in progress, apprehend rapists, that sort of thing.

"In 1985 Domino's Pizza guys were being robbed. The offender was calling in for pizza; then when the driver showed up, he'd put a gun under the guy's chin. To catch him I posed as a Domino's delivery man. I got 'Officer of the Year' for that.

"Our unit would cover burglaries, too, and if another agency called looking for a violent fugitive, we'd go after him. When the Rollover Rapist was on the loose back in 1985, we saturated the area looking for him and we caught him. We'd use female decoys and simulate a car breakdown to see what happened, that sort of thing.

"I've hidden in dumpsters and gotten into a few close calls. One time I was trying to put a 'bird dog' on a rape suspect's car—that's a tracking device. I crawled under the car, which was in his driveway at the time, but before I finished, he came walking out and got into his car. He almost ran me over: he started to back up, but my partners came and distracted him by asking for directions. I was able to get out in time.

"That wasn't the first time we staged distractions. One time two cops had an accident—they ran their cars into each other—so we could distract a suspect and go in and get him.

"From 1983 to 1988, I worked with the SWAT teams. We had two teams, entry teams of four guys each. We'd go into buildings after barricaded subjects or to carry out search warrants or on narcotics busts.

"When the president came to town, we guarded him. At the funeral for a cop, we did the security. We'd be on the rooftops, making sure that no one was there ready to fire into the crowd.

"The camaraderie in this work is unbelievable. There were fourteen of us, and every one would lay down their life for you. I knew that if I was running down the hallway chasing someone, they'd be right behind me.

"But those were rough days, and there was a lot of drinking after work to deal with the stress. I think back to what I did: I was a fool, I was young, and I had the attitude I would never get hurt. I've been asked to go back to the SWAT team as sergeant, but I turned it down.

"My wife didn't appreciate my being called in the middle of the night. I was glad to move on to another assignment."

The Ride of Your Life

If you are willing to sign an agreement that the police department will not be held responsible in case of any "incidents," you could find yourself riding shotgun in a police car. Almost every department across the country allows what are called observer rides. Interested parties spend a whole shift with an officer of the law, going out on any calls that happen to come in.

What would your night be like? Here are some of the possibilities: "in progress calls," "delayed calls," domestic violence, robberies, drug busts, even homicides.

All sorts of people take advantage of observer rides—people just like yourself, law and criminal justice students, writers, career investigators, and even private citizens concerned about their community.

To arrange an observer ride, telephone the media relations department or the public information office of your local police department.

Fire Investigation

Fire investigators arrive at the scene of a fire and try to determine how it started. Although there are many types of fires, anything from a trash basket fire to a devastating forest fire, they all fall into just two categories: accidental or criminal.

An accident happens unintentionally, such as when someone falls asleep smoking a cigarette or oily rags carelessly left in a corner suddenly ignite. Criminal fires are fires that were set on purpose. This is called *arson* and is punishable by law. Fires caused by bombs also fall under the category of criminal fires.

There are several motives for arson, including spite, revenge, anger, and fraud. The most common kind of arson fraud happens when someone's business is going bad and they decide to "sell it back to the insurance company." They hire someone to burn it or burn it themselves, and then they try to collect on their insurance.

Fire investigators check into both accidental and criminal fires. The engine company first goes out and does the firefighting. Once the fire has been put out, the lieutenant on the scene will take a look at it to try to understand why the fire started. The lieutenant will include this information in the written report. If the loss is above $5000 or so, or there is a suspicion that the fire wasn't accidental, the fire investigator comes in to do a more in-depth check.

Fire investigators look at fires as big puzzles with lots of little pieces that have to be put together in order to make sense. The fire investigator likes to be at the scene when the fire is still burning. A fire in progress can give a lot of information. Sometimes it's possible to tell from the color of the flame or the smoke what caused the fire: When wood burns, the smoke is dark with a brown tinge. But if you add gasoline, fire burns with a lot of black smoke. Arriving in time to watch how the fire reacts to water can also yield some clues. If the fire doesn't go right out when soaked down but instead keeps coming back, then there's a good chance a fuel was used.

Fire investigators also look at what part of the building is burning. If it's a large house and the fire's burning in the living room and kitchen, for example, and then during the fire-fighting operation the fire spreads back to the bedrooms, the investigators can get an idea where it first started and focus their investigation there.

After the fire is out, everything looks black, but the debris still reveals clues. Fire investigators can shovel through the mess and look for burn patterns. They can see which side of a piece of wood or what part of the carpeting is more deeply burned.

They look at wiring, fuse boxes, and circuit breaker boxes. They also talk to the firefighters and ask what they saw. Were the doors unlocked? Was anyone running away? Was there broken glass lying inside, or was it blown outside by the fire?

Do You Have What It Takes?

Fire investigation is not for the faint of heart. There are many dangers involved. These days many materials in our homes are made from plastic, and plastic is made with chemicals. So after a fire when the temperature cools down, fumes start escaping. Because of this fire investigators must wear masks with filters to protect their lungs.

Shoveling through the debris in a burned out building is also dangerous. A fire weakens all the structure's supports, and roofs can suddenly collapse, walls can cave in, and floors can give way.

Fire investigators sometimes have to work with the police or even go into court to testify. Because they are often called to give evidence in court, these professionals need to have a knowledge of the law and court procedure. They must also have good writing skills, because the reports they write might be read in court. And of course, they must have good speaking skills to give convincing testimony.

Fire investigators get their satisfaction from figuring out how fires started. They like to be able to look back and say that they know now that the toaster oven went bad or someone broke into the house and poured gasoline on the carpet.

But the frustration comes from not being able to prove who did it and to see the arsonist caught. Evidence gets destroyed in the fire. Evidence of how it was done and why it was done is usually not enough to get a conviction.

Training for Fire Investigators

Fire investigators must first go through regular firefighter training and put in their time as a firefighter. Once they are approved to become an investigator, the training is an ongoing process. They study fire behavior, chemistry, court procedures, and how to handle evidence. They attend special classes at colleges and fire academies and also go through internships with seasoned investigators.

Not all fire investigators work for fire departments, though. Some with the appropriate training and experience find work with insurance companies or private investigation firms.

Salaries for Fire Investigators

The salaries for this specialty vary from department to department. In some departments investigators who carry a firefighter rank would earn the same as a firefighter. The salary increases 10 to 15 percent with promotions to the lieutenant level. All firefighters within a department receive the same benefits, vacation time, generous sick leave, and a full retirement pension after twenty years of service.

Bob Lemons, Fire Investigator, and Holly, Accelerant Detection Canine

Some lucky fire investigators get to work with dogs trained to sniff out *accelerants*—substances that burn quickly, such as gasoline or diesel fuel.

Bob Lemons is a fire investigator for the Boca Raton, Florida fire/rescue department. He is also the handler of Holly, an accelerant detection canine. Holly is a part of Bob's family, and when she's not working, she's at home with the Lemonses and their two children.

Bob talks about his work:

"Once I got on the fire department, I got a broader view of what goes on; and while I do like riding the rescue trucks with the sirens and the lights, the fire investigation at the end seemed more interesting. I watched the investigators come in at a fire, and I asked a lot of questions: Why are you doing this? Why are you looking here? What are you looking for? I was persistent. After your supervisors get to know you and see that it's not just idle curiosity, they help you along.

"How I got involved with Holly almost came about by accident. I was sitting in the fire station and saw a magazine article about one of these dogs, an accelerant detection canine. That was back in '89 or '90. These dogs have only been around since '88. It was a new twist on what I was already interested in. I spoke to the chief and said, 'This is what I would like you to do. I'd like you to send me to the Maine State Police Canine Academy in Portland for five weeks, with a dog, to learn how to investigate fires.'

"He thought that was the funniest thing he'd ever heard. But I showed him the article, did some more research, found out the success rate, how good they were, and then I went back to my chief. He realized a dog like Holly would be a good tool. So in 1990 I started looking for a dog. Holly was donated by a local family for this job. Labradors are good for this kind of work. She was three at the time.

"I looked at several dogs before I found Holly. The dog has to have the right temperament. You want a dog who is very social, who likes to be around people. She has to be curious and have a good nose. She can't be afraid of loud noises or new environments. And she can't be afraid of going into places where the footing isn't always sturdy. Holly tromps right through. She enjoys her work.

"Holly is trained to go in after a fire and search for residue of a flammable or combustible liquid, such as gasoline, diesel fuel, or lighter fluid. When she finds something, she sits and signals us. We collect the samples from where she's indicated and send them to the lab. Her success rate is very good. Even if the equipment can't pick it up, Holly can.

"Often an arsonist will stay near the fire to watch the firefighters at work. I can take Holly on a leash and walk her through the crowd watching the fire. If the arsonist is hanging around, Holly will be able to find him because he will still have the smell of gasoline on his hands and clothes. I'll take her through quickly, and when I see that she's getting ready to alert, I'll pull her away so we don't tip off the arsonist. I'll then signal the police, who will be watching from nearby. They've been able to make quite a few arrests this way. All the arsonist knows is that a dog walked by and a few seconds later the police are on him.

"But we don't always assume that there was arson involved just because the dog sits down and signals us. There are a lot of reasons why flammable liquids are kept in the house. People might store their charcoal lighter fluid inside, or gasoline for the lawn mower. Holly can find the fuel, but she doesn't know if it was there legitimately. That's where the human fire investigators have to take over."

The Training of an Accelerant Detection Canine

Holly has been trained on a food reward system. The only time she eats is when she finds something. Now that doesn't mean she goes without her regular meals if there are no fires to investigate. On her days off, Bob takes a little dropper of flammable liquid the chemist has prepared and puts a few drops down in the driveway or in his house. Then he puts her in a work mode and has her begin her search. When she finds it, she gets to eat. This goes on every single day. No little treats or between-meal snacks.

"There's a good reason why we use a food reward," Bob explains. "A lot of dogs are rewarded with playtime. A drug dog will find a suitcase with drugs in it and will start biting and scratching it. The handler will bring out a ball or towel and praise the dog, and then the dog will grab the towel and release the article.

"But in a fire setting, all that playing would disturb the evidence. We need a dog that will alert by sitting very still.

"There were five steps to Holly's training. First, through repetition, we imprinted Holly with the odor. Just as you teach a dog to sit over and over, Holly was taught that when she smells this odor [gasoline or any other accelerant], she'll get a food reward. We start with an odor contained in a can, but so she doesn't sit down every time she sees a can, we also put cans out that are empty and odorless.

"Then we put in the alert. It's a two-step passive alert—the 'sit' and 'show me.' Holly learns that in order to get fed, she must find the odor, then sit. She comes in, sniffs around the can, sits down, and then I say, 'Show me.' Holly will put her nose directly where she smells the odor. We teach her this because in a fire scene everything is all black, and we have to know exactly what piece of debris has the flammable liquid on it.

"Now we transfer this process to a larger area. Instead of containing the odor in cans, we put it on the can lids, which we spread out on the ground. She then learns to check on the floor. When she's working, she makes a sound like a pig rooting around, snuffling as she sniffs the area. We also use four or five other odorless lids. She'll see the silver thing on the ground and will sniff until she finds the one with the odor. Then she'll sit and be fed.

"Next we take her to both 'hot' fire scenes, where we know she will find something, and 'cold' fire scenes, where we know she won't. We want to make sure she understands she won't always find something every time she comes to a fire scene.

"Finally we do a blind test to make sure she really is finding the odor, that it's not just coincidence. A chemist prepares five sample cans. He numbers them from 1 to 5 and puts burnt debris in each of them. But he will only put a drop of accelerant in one of the cans, and he's the only one who knows which can it is. Then we take the lids off and let Holly sniff. The chemist checks his log to see if the can she alerted was the right one."

What Bob's Job Is Really Like

"You meet a lot of people and interact with different agencies, the local police, the state fire marshall, the federal people. And it's always a big pleasure working with Holly. She's a good partner. But she has her moods, just like we do. There are days you don't feel like working, and the same holds true for Holly. Sometimes at fire scenes or—it will always be when it's important—say, at a demonstration for a fire official, Holly will just look around and say, 'Not today.' You can tell she's just going through the motions.

"The rewards of this job really are few and far between. That's because you can know how a fire started, know that it was arson, but you can't prove it in a court of law. A lot of times, you learn that the insurance company had to pay the claim even though you know the owner did it. Only about 4 percent of arsonists ever get caught and convicted. You get frustrated, but inside you know you did the best job you could do. You did your part."

Attorneys at Law
For the Defense

Before there were F. Lee Bailey, Robert Shapiro, and Johnny Cocheran, TV's Perry Mason was probably the best known lawyer in this country. His clients were always innocent, he alway got them off, and he always nabbed the real criminal in the process.

Again, real life does not always follow the imagination of television writers. If you decide to pursue a career in criminal law, many of your clients will not be innocent, and you might not be able to get them all off. Some you'd even rather not represent. But in our justice system everyone is innocent until proven guilty, and everyone is entitled to legal defense.

Criminal lawyers operate their own practices, work for private law firms, or represent clients under the auspices of the public defender's office.

For the Prosecution

For every F. Lee Bailey there's a Marcia Clark. Lawyers who work for state attorneys general, prosecutors, and courts play a key role in the criminal justice system. At the federal level attorneys investigate cases for the Department of Justice or other agencies. Also, lawyers at every government level help develop programs, draft laws, interpret legislation, establish enforcement procedures, and argue civil and criminal cases on behalf of the government.

No matter the setting, whether acting as advocate or prosecutor, all attorneys interpret the law and apply it to specific situations. This requires research and communication abilities.

Lawyers perform in-depth research into the purposes behind the applicable laws and into judicial decisions that have been applied to those laws under circumstances similar to those currently faced by the client. Although all lawyers continue to make use of conventional law libraries to prepare cases, some supplement their search of the old-fashioned printed sources with computer software packages that automatically search the legal literature and identify legal tests that may be relevant to a specific subject.

In litigation that involves many supporting documents, lawyers may also use computers to organize and index the material. Lawyers then communicate to others the information obtained by research.

The Training You'll Need

To practice law in the courts of any state or other jurisdiction, a person must be licensed, or admitted to its bar, under rules established by the jurisdiction's highest court. Nearly all jurisdictions require that applicants for admission to the bar pass a written bar examination. Most also require applicants to pass a separate written ethics examination. Lawyers who have been admitted to the bar in one jurisdiction occasionally may be admitted to the bar in another without taking an examination if they meet that jurisdiction's standards of good moral character and have a specified period of legal experience.

Federal courts and agencies set their own qualifications for those practicing before them.

To qualify for the bar examination in most states, an applicant must complete at least three years of college and graduate from a law school approved by the American Bar Association (ABA) or the proper state authorities. (ABA approval signifies that the law school, particularly its library and faculty, meets certain standards developed by the association to promote quality legal education.)

Seven states accept the study of law in a law office or in combination with study of law school; only California accepts the study of law by correspondence as qualifying for taking the bar examination.

Several states require registration and approval of students by the State Board of Law Examiners, either before they enter law school or during the early years of legal study.

The required college and law school education usually takes seven years of full-time study after high school: four years of undergraduate study followed by three years in law school. Although some law schools accept a very small number of students after three years of college, most require applicants to have a bachelor's degree. To meet the needs of students who can attend only part-time, a number of law schools have night or part-time divisions, which usually require four years of study.

Acceptance by most law schools depends on the applicant's ability to demonstrate an aptitude for the study of law, usually through good undergraduate grades, the Law School Admission Test (LSAT), the quality of the applicant's undergraduate school, any prior work experience, and sometimes a personal interview. However, law schools vary in the weight that they place on each of these factors.

All law schools approved by the ABA require that applicants take the LSAT. Nearly all law schools require that applicants have certified transcripts sent to the Law School Data Assembly Service. This service then sends applicants' LSAT scores and their standardized records of college grades to the law schools of their choice. Both this service and the LSAT are administered by the Law School Admission Services.

Graduates receive the degree of juris doctor (J.D.) or bachelor of law (LL.B.) as the first professsional degree. Advanced law degrees may be desirable for those planning to specialize, do research, or teach. Some law students pursue joint degree programs, which generally require an additional year. Joint degree programs are offered in a number of areas, including law and business administration and law and public administration.

Earnings for Lawyers

Contrary to the experience of John Grisham's hero in *The Firm*, annual salaries of beginning lawyers in private industry average about $36,600. But top graduates from the nation's best law schools start in some cases at over $80,000 a year. In the federal government annual starting salaries for attorneys in 1993 were about $27,800 or $33,600, depending upon academic and personal qualifications.

Factors affecting the salaries offered to new graduates include the academic record; the type, size, and location of employer; and the specialized educational background desired.

Salaries of experienced attorneys also vary widely according to the type, size, and location of their employer. The average salary of the most experienced lawyers in private industry in 1992 was over $134,000, but some senior lawyers who were partners in the nation's top law firms earned over $1 million. General attorneys in the federal government averaged around $62,200 a year in 1993.

Lawyers on salary receive increases as they assume greater responsibility. Lawyers starting their own practice may need to work part-time in other occupations during the first years to supplement their income. Their income usually grows as their practice develops. Lawyers who are partners in law firms generally earn more than those who practice alone.

Private Investigation

In the 1980s TV viewers watched the exploits of *Magnum, PI*; readers of Sue Grafton's novels still follow the adventures of detective Kinsey Milhone. The field of private investigation can be exciting and glamorous; it can also be tedious and dull. For every undercover operation there are hundreds of hours spent on the telephone or surfing the 'Net, and an equal number sitting in a car at a stakeout, sipping a mug of cold coffee.

Settings for PIs

Private investigators can work for detective agencies or go it solo. They also find work either as employees or as independent contractors with insurance companies, shopping malls, hotels, and other private concerns. They can work undercover, infiltrating a ring of thieves, or sit at a desk doing background checks. They sniff out shoplifters, finger employees who are stealing, or locate missing persons. They also act as bodyguards or security guards.

The Earnings You Can Expect

James Rockford of TV's *The Rockford Files* asked for $200 a day plus expenses. In real life PIs bill their clients anywhere from $25 to $125 per hour, depending upon the type of investigation. Beginning investigators working for a private firm might start out only in the teens. Experienced investigators can earn anywhere from $20,000 a year to $300,000. Earnings vary greatly depending upon the employer, specialty, and geographic area. Those who own their own firms and are doing well make at the higher end; those who work as store detective, for example, see the bottom of the scale.

The Training You'll Need

Most employers prefer to hire high school graduates, and a college degree, especially in criminal justice or related fields, is becoming more and more the preferred background for some companies. A growing number of states are enacting mandatory training programs for investigators. In 1993, there were forty-two states, along with the District of Columbia, that required licenses for private investigators. In most cases it is the state police department that issues the licenses, but requirements vary widely.

You can get entry-level training on the job. Many come to the profession from related fields, as former police officers or government agents.

Undercover Work

Twenty-plus years ago Joe Nickell began his career as a private investigator for a world famous detective agency. He has since taken another track and is now a paranormal investigator. (You can read more about this unusual career in chapter 5.) But he got his start doing surveillance, background checks, and some dicey undercover work.

"I did mostly undercover jobs. Between those jobs there was all sorts of surveillance work and background checks. I even did body-guarding for a politician. But primarily I was a part of the cadre of young investigators doing the more dangerous undercover work.

"We would work in a company's warehouse—as a stock clerk, shipper/receiver, mail clerk, forklift driver—wherever they could slip us in. Our job was really to become aware of and infiltrate theft rings operating there. We'd set them up and bust them. The work was done privately and secretly. We'd assure the owners that we could get rid of the problem without the whole story coming out.

"If the story did come out, it would result in bad morale. The employees would not be happy that the bosses had sent spies in.

"The police would not be involved. The company would handle it themselves, fire the men, and hope to keep the thieves out.

"Plus, the detective agency would not want its men to have to go to court. Once you did and you were identified, it would mean the end of your undercover career. The agency would want to be able to use us again and again, not just one time.

"I also did surveillance work, staking out a place where we had undercover guys. Or at times we'd be on the phone, just checking up on background and character of different people.

"Unlike some of the guys, who hated doing any of the office work, I would go looking for the general work whenever I was between undercover assignments.

"When you were on an undercover assignment, you got your paycheck with the other factory or warehouse workers. Then your agency would make up the difference in your pay. You'd also get extra danger pay on top of that."

Insurance Fraud

Joe Nickell also worked on insurance fraud cases. "I was assigned to do surveillance on someone who was claiming he had a back injury. We staked out his house and watched him work on his car, photographing every move. He was bending over, darting up the steps two at a time. We documented it all."

Art Forgeries

This is not a field to enter lightly. One must have a serious background in art, either as an artist, art gallery owner, or museum curator. Rarely is authenticating art a full-time position. It often comes as a sideline to regular duties in the above mentioned occupations.

Matthew Carone is the owner of the Carone Gallery, a prestigious establishment in Fort Lauderdale, Florida. He handles mainly contemporary art: American, some European, and some Latin American paintings and sculpture.

How his reputation became established was, in part, the result of discovering an art forgery. "When you're starting, you have to establish yourself as a serious gallery. I happened to do it by way of master graphics. I got involved with original prints, not reproductions, but very serious Picassos, very serious Cézanne and Matisse prints, and I got a reputation for that in the early years. This made it easier for me to then work one-on-one with important artists because they knew of my seriousness.

"Many of the sources for these prints happened to be in Europe, which allowed me to go there every two or three months. The most important dealers in Europe met once a month to discuss what was happening in the art world, what was new, what was fake, that sort of thing. As it turned out, I had discovered a Picasso fake and got a lot of mileage and publicity through that.

"I'm color blind, but I became 'value sensitive.' I can see the value of a color, the lightness or darkness, more so than a person with normal color vision. The ink used for this one Picasso was called an ivory black, which is the blackest of blacks, but I knew that the original had a warmer black. On the basis of that, I knew there was something wrong, so I went to Paris and showed it to a very important Picasso dealer. He said to me, 'Mr. Carone, if you had showed me this print framed, under glass, I would have said it was OK; but you're right, this is a fake.' This led me to Picasso's biggest dealer, but my biggest mistake was when he said we must show this to Picasso—I should have insisted that I go along with that print, but I didn't do that. They sent it to him, and Picasso did send it back to me with a 'Faux'—'fake'—with a line through it. But Picasso signed it, meaning, 'Picasso says "Faux," ' " so it then achieved some value. Anything he put his name to had value, and the 'Faux' print became an interesting thing to see. A prominent international auction house said that the print was very good, so whoever the artist was, he had a lot of talent. The fake was terrific.

"The FBI, of course, got involved with this; they had an idea who he was, but it was never pursued because it's very difficult to prove. They never found out.

"This event came at that time of my life when I was getting involved seriously, and it gave me a new level of importance. Everybody started banging on my door wanting me to look at their Picassos. Now over the years, I've developed a clientele that comes to me for particulars."

Further Information
Police Work

Information about entrance requirements for police work may be obtained from federal, state, and local civil service commissions or police departments.

Contact any Office of Personnel Management Job Information Center for pamphlets providing general information and instructions for submitting an application for jobs as Treasury Department special agents, drug enforcement agents, FBI special agents, or U.S. marshals. Look under "U.S. Government—Office of Personnel Management" in your telephone directory to obtain a local telephone number.

For information about police work in general, contact:

International Union of Police Associations
1016 Duke Street
Alexandria, VA 22314

Fire Investigation

For information about professional qualifications and a list of two- and four-year degree programs in fire science or fire prevention, contact:

National Fire Protection Association
Batterymarch Park
Quincy, MA 02269

Legal Practice

The ABA annually publishes *A Review of Legal Education in the United States*, which provides detailed information on each of the 177 law schools approved by the ABA, state requirements for admission to legal practice, a directory of state bar examination administrators, and other information on legal education. Single copies are free from the ABA, but there is a fee for multiple copies. Free information on the bar examination, financial aid for law students, and law as a career may also be obtained from:

Member Services
American Bar Association
541 North Fairbanks Court
Chicago, IL 60611-3314

Information on the LSAT, the Law School Data Assembly Service, applying to law school, and financial aid for law students may be obtained from:

Law School Admission Services
P. O. Box 40
Newtown, PA 18940

The specific requirements for admission to the bar in a particular state or other jurisdiction may also be obtained at the state capital from the clerk of the Supreme Court or the administrator of the state Board of Law Examiners.

Private Investigation

For information on a career as a private detective or investigator, contact:

International Security and Detective Alliance
P. O. Box 6303
Corpus Christi, TX 78466-6303

CHAPTER FIVE

Unsolved Mysteries

D o you believe in ghosts and spirits and haunted houses? What about ESP and psychokinesis? UFOs? The Loch Ness Monster? Bigfoot?

Did you see *Ghostbusters* or *Close Encounters of the Third Kind*? Do you watch *The X-Files* or *Sightings*? Do books by Isaac Asimov or Arthur Clarke excite and intrigue you?

Maybe, or maybe not. When it comes to the realm of the paranormal, there are usually three sides on which people align themselves. There are the believers, those who cannot be shaken from their stand. Then there are the nonbelievers, those who would never be convinced. Finally, there are those in between, the show-me group. They keep an open mind but would need hard evidence to move them off the fence.

The strong beliefs of some, either for or against, have led to some interesting careers. But be forewarned—job opportunities in this area are few and far between. Only a small fraction of dedicated believers or debunkers have been able to carve a niche for themselves in this controversial territory.

What Does It All Mean?

Every discipline has its own jargon. Before we forge ahead, it's a good idea to have a few definitions in our arsenal.

PARANORMAL is a word used to describe activity outside or beyond the reach of present-day scientific thought or knowledge.

PARAPSYCHOLOGY is the study of psychic phenomena.

PSYCHIC PHENOMENA when referred to in relation to the human mind, psychic phenomena usually falls into two categories: *extrasensory perception (ESP)* and *psychokinesis (PK)*.

ESP is the ability to obtain information without the benefit of the senses. It is usually split into two subcategories: *telepathy*, the ability to perceive someone else's thoughts; and *clairvoyance*, the ability to sense an object or event outside the range of the senses.

Zener Cards were specially designed to test ESP ability. A deck consists of a series of five cards, each card having one of five symbols—a star, square, circle, plus sign, and three wavy lines.

PK is the ability of the mind to influence animate or inanimate matter without the use of any known physical or sensory means. In other words, it is the ability to move or alter matter by thought alone.

PK includes: *telekinesis*, the ability to move objects; *levitation*, the ability to overcome gravity and rise or float in the air; *materialization*, the ability to cause a spirit or other nonphysical being to take a bodily form; *poltergeist activity*, mysterious events such as rappings, overturned furniture, and flying objects; and *paranormal healing*, the ability to cure disease or affliction by no known scientific means.

SPIRITUALISM is a system of beliefs focused on efforts to communicate with the dead or with spirits. **Channelers** facilitate communications between the earthly and spirit worlds. Some channelers also attempt contact with extraterrestrials or spirits from ancient mythical societies, as well as with the recently deceased. Channelers are also sometimes referred to as **mediums**.

Automatic writing is a way for spirits to communicate with the living. A medium or channeler will hold a pen and pad of paper, then enter a trance. This allows the spirit to express his or her thoughts using the medium's hand.

A Little History

Interest in psychic phenomena can be traced back to early times. The first modern organizations to investigate such phenomena were the British Society for Psychical Research, founded in 1881, and the American Society for Psychical Research, founded in 1885.

Much of the early investigation conducted by these two groups was unscientific and anecdotal in nature. J. B. Rhine, a psychologist at Duke University in Durham, North Carolina, wanted to change the approach and methods used. He began his work investigating parapsychology in 1927. In the course of his work, Rhine coined the term *extrasensory perception*. Duke eventually allowed him to split from the psychology department and form the first parapsychological laboratory in the country. That was in 1935. A little more than fifteen years ago, the parapsychology department and Duke University parted ways. But those carrying on Rhine's work did not want to let it die. They soon formed the Institute for Parapsychology, which is also located in Durham, North Carolina. (Their address is in the appendix.)

The Controversy

The majority of scientists outside the field of parapsychology do not accept the existence of psychic phenomena. As a result they do not accept the discipline of parapsychology: in order to study something, there has to be something there to study.

The most weighty criticism launched against parapsychologists is that of fraud. Rhine himself discovered that one of his researchers had been faking results. (The man was dismissed.) Parapsychologists counter this charge by saying that they do well in policing their own ranks.

Another charge is that parapsychologists are not trained to tell whether a subject is committing fraud. Even amateur magicians have been known to fool investigators. Parapsychologists insist that this type of fraud happens only in an insignificant number of cases.

Another major criticism is that for ESP, PK, and other phenomena to be true, basic physical laws would have to be broken. To counter that, some parapsychologists believe that breakthroughs in particle physics may one day provide explanations for such phenomena. Others feel that paranormal activity operates outside the realm of science.

Toward the end of his life, the great psychologist Carl Jung suggested that the deepest layers of the unconscious function independently of the laws of space, time, and causality, allowing for paranormal phenomena.

Other charges against parapsychology include shoddy experimental design, incorrect statistical interpretations, and misread data.

A study in 1988, conducted by the National Research Council, maintained that no scientific research in the past 130 years had proven the existence of parapsychological phenomena. The council, however, did find anomalies in some experiments that they could not readily explain. Parapsychologists claim that the study was biased because the members of the research committee were nonbelievers.

Joe Nickell, Paranormal Investigator

Joe Nickell is one of the very few paid paranormal investigators in the country. He's a staff member of the Committee for the Scientific Investigation of Claims of the Paranormal (CSICOP), which is based at the Center for Inquiry, a nonprofit organization in Buffalo, New York.

He's had an interesting and colorful career and has worked as a private investigator (see chapter 4), a professional stage magician at the Houdini Hall of Fame (under the stage names Janus the Magician and Mendell the Mentalist), a blackjack dealer, a riverboat manager, a newspaper stringer, a historical and literary investigator, and a writer of articles and books. (See a listing at the end of the chapter.) He has also managed to find time to earn a bachelor's, a master's, and a Ph. D. degree, all in English literature, all from the University of Kentucky at Lexington.

"I grew up with magic in the household; my father was an amateur magician. I am largely self-taught, but also a retired magician helped me some.

"During my career at Houdini, before I went on to be an investigator, I met James Randi—The Amazing Randi—and he was doing a lot of paranormal investigations. I thought what he did was interesting and exciting, exposing psychics.

"Pretty soon thereafter, I think in 1972, I had the opportunity to investigate a haunted house called Mackenzie House, an historic building in Toronto. There were various phenomena happening late at night there. The caretakers would hear footsteps going up and down the stairs—when no one was there. There were other sounds, too; Mackenzie's printing press, for example.

"I found that the sounds were all illusions. They were real sounds, but they were coming from the building next door. The buildings were only forty inches apart, and the other building had a staircase made of iron that ran parallel to the Mackenzie House stairway. Whenever anybody went up and down the stairs next door, it sounded as if it was coming from within the Mackenzie House. The interesting thing to me was that no one had figured this out for ten years.

"I was doing a lot of writing at the time, and still am, but at the beginning I discovered that the paranormal was a theme that I kept turning to again and again. There were so many intriguing questions. In the early seventies there were all kinds of claims—of psychics, of the 'ancient astronaut,' theories about the Bermuda Triangle. It's kind of all passé now, but at the time I thought of them as burning questions.

"I've always been skeptical, not meaning debunking, just meaning 'prove it to me.' I began to investigate paranormal claims. I was in the Yukon Territory working as a blackjack dealer and would occasionally do a newspaper piece. One day these guys were all claiming that they could use their dowsing wands to find gold. So I said, 'Talk is cheap. Would you do it under control-test conditions?' They agreed. I put gold nuggets in some boxes padded with cotton; other boxes had nothing in them, some had fool's gold, some had nuts and bolts. I scrambled them all up, and even I didn't know when I picked a box out of the sack what was in it. The only way they would have known was if there had been any psychic power at work—and of course they failed the test miserably. I ended up writing an article about the experiment.

"I did investigations all through college. Whenever I heard about something interesting, I'd pursue it myself. The next big investigation, where I made a name for myself, was with the Shroud of Turin. On my own I decided that the image on the shroud, which was supposed to be impossible to duplicate because it's a negative image and that no forger in the Middle Ages could duplicate, could indeed be duplicated. I showed a very easy way to duplicate it, using a very simple process. That I published in several magazines, including one in *Popular Photography*, which got me on every newsstand in America.

"From there and other publications I attracted the notice of this committee. The Committee for Scientific Investigation of Claims of the Paranormal was founded in 1976. We're having our twentieth anniversary now. The committee's founder was Paul Hurtz, who worked very closely with James Randi, Isaac Asimov, Carl Sagan.

"There was a feeling that this paranormal stuff was being hyped on TV and in the tabloids and there was no voice to speak counter to it. CSICOP was set up to investigate, not to dismiss out of hand, not to start out to debunk, but simply to investigate claims of the paranormal. And if that meant debunking, so be it.

"I had volunteered for years for CSICOP; then in 1995 I was hired full-time. The center needed a detective, a magician, a writer, and a researcher, and by hiring me they got all of them in one.

"I'm sort of a magic detective. Parapsychologists really believe that there is some power of the mind to read people's thoughts or divine the future or whatever. In spite of what you might have read, though, there is no scientific evidence for any of this. There have been plenty of claims, but when the claims have been scrutinized, they've been found not to pan out. Poor research methodology, or tricksters using slight-of-hand. And that's where I come in.

"But the phrase 'try to debunk' is very loaded. We go out to investigate. Invariably, we also do end up debunking.

"I was asked to be a consultant on *Unsolved Mysteries*, for example. Most viewers think of the program as a documentary, but in fact it's just entertainment. They don't care whether they tell the truth or not. That's often the case. I've worked with them many times, and often they've left out important details, making it look much more serious; and if you question them on it, they say, 'Well, after all, the name of our program is Unsolved *Mysteries*.'

"One question *Unsolved Mysteries* asked me to explain involved some miracle photographs that were taken at a Virgin Mary site in Kentucky. They sent me copies of the photographs, and I was able to duplicate all the effects and explain them. The pictures were made by some girls—Polaroids that showed unusual things, they thought. The girls had attempted to take a picture of the sun— when the picture came out, they had a picture of a doorway with an arched top and straight sides, flooded with light. The doorway to heaven. In fact, that shape was the shape of the camera's lens opening—a light-flooded silhouette of that aperture. At the bottom of a few of the pictures were what they thought were angel wings. In fact, those were due to light leaking into the cartridge.

"The most puzzling was a picture that had a faint image super-imposed over the picture of the girls. It was some sort of chart. I kept saying it didn't sound miraculous, it sounded very human. I tried to figure out how it could get on there. CSICOP let me have fifty dollars to buy film with. No sooner than I put in a film pack, it ejected a protector card. On the other side of the card, when I turned it over, there was the chart. I had to laugh. When the show aired, they reported all my findings, which was very gratifying given their reputation for leaving things out.

"Another case I was involved with was a haunted Japanese restaurant in Atlanta. First, Dr. William Roll, a parapsychologist based there, was on *Unsolved Mysteries* to investigate the phenomenon. One of the things he did was to take in a magnetometer. You ask yourself, "Why is Dr. Roll taking a magnetometer in? Is there a body of scientific evidence that ghosts are influenced by magnetometers?" No, there is not. There is not such a reputable body of scientific knowledge. But often self-styled ghost hunters take in fancy-sounding equipment, and if they get any type of glitches or movement, they assume it must be the ghost doing it.

"They can make fools of themselves. The manager of that very same restaurant told me that he knew that the magnetometer was simply responding to the iron metal in the pipes in the walls. The result of our investigation was that the ghost was mostly a lot of hysteria and hype and some of the employees playing pranks on one another.

"We're often accused of being debunkers, as if we start out to do that. But here's the proof that we don't dismiss out of hand. If we did, we would not go to the Georgia restaurant to do an investigation. We'd say that it was just too silly to bother with. In fact, we do the investigations, but we get different results. Why? Because we don't take in silly equipment. We go in and interview people; we look for evidence; we look for causes. We got a girl to actually confess privately that the reason the lights went on and off, which is something the bartender told us about, was that when he wasn't looking she would reach around and flip the switch. She had great fun doing that for some time.

"CSICOP doesn't just parachute me in whenever there's a rumor of something. We're nonprofit and most of our money is donated, so we have to be very careful with how we spend it. Some of our funding comes from subscriptions to our journal, the *Skeptical Inquirer*.

"When I do an investigation for a TV show, they usually pay for us to fly down there. I've been a guest on a lot of different shows:

Larry King Live, Sally Jessy Raphael, Maury Povich, Charles Grodin.
So often I'm the token skeptic. They put on the believers, the UFO
abductees and so forth, and I get a minute at the end to say, 'Bah
humbug.'

"But I once got to test a psychic on the *Jerry Springer* show. It was
a lot of fun. There were three psychics on, doing all sorts of readings,
telling people about themselves. There's a trick to this: it's called
cold reading. What you do is fish for info. You start off vague; then
if the person gives you a little feedback—maybe he looks suprised,
or he nods in agreement—you pursue that. If he shakes his head or
says, 'No, I don't have a brother,' then you pursue that. You actually
can narrow your choices, and by the time you're through, you've
convinced them that you know all about them. And if you've missed
a few, you don't back off them. You say, 'Well, I think you will meet
someone named Robert, and it's going to happen soon.'

"I was brought on as the skeptic to see if these people were really
psychic. I said, 'I have three envelopes containing a simple three-
letter word. And I also have a check for $1000. The check is yours
if you can guess or divine all three of the three-letter words.' Two
of the psychics refused to cooperate. The third, who called himself
Mr. B of ESP, the World's Greatest Psychic, agreed to be tested.
Well, he failed the test. I had to tear up the check. There was a
mixture of booing and applause from the audience.

"I am most interested in the investigative aspect of my work. I
like solving the mysteries. That's the most rewarding part. I've never
really been stumped. That doesn't mean that I know the answer to
every mystery in the world. I've looked back through history, and
sometimes I've been able to find the solution to a long-ago puzzle.

"For example, there's the story about the disappearance of Oliver
Lerch. As the story went, in South Bend, Indiana, in the 1890s,
young Oliver was sent out to the well to get some water on Christmas
Eve while everyone was gathered around the hearth and playing
the piano. No sooner did he leave on his errand than the family
heard him crying for help. Some thought he might even have said,
'They've got me.'

"They picked up the lantern and ran outside, following Oliver's tracks through the snow. They got halfway to the well, whereupon the tracks ended abruptly. No sign of Oliver. A great mystery. How do you explain it?

"The story has been published in slews of different books and magazines on unsolved mysteries. Well, I did a little further investigation, and I found there was no such family as the Lerches. I did a deed search and found that no family named Lerch had ever owned any property in that area. Some of the stories claimed that the incident was still in the police files. Well, the police say they've never heard of it. No such story. Oliver Lerch never disappeared; Oliver Lerch never even existed. In fact, the story is more or less a plagiarized version of an old Ambrose Bierce horror story called " 'Charles Ashmore's Trail.' "

Some Advice from Joe Nickell

"I think you should read as much of the literature as possible, particularly the skeptical literature. You're going to be misled by a lot of the believers. They'll tell you stories that simply aren't true. Their books are full of the fake Oliver Lerch stories. And it's not they who expose them, it's us. Our journal, *The Skeptical Inquirer*, frequently reviews books and lists articles. That would be a good starting point.

"Then it would be useful to learn something about magic. Not that everyone has to be a magician, but some of us are. It's useful in understanding how people can be fooled and what the different tricks are.

"In addition to magic, depending upon the area you're most interested in, journalism, psychology, and astronomy would be useful. One of our people is with NASA, another with *Aviation Science* magazine. Psychology would be very good investigating people who feel they're possessed or haunted or have been abducted by aliens. There are many different fields. We all count on each other and share. An investigation often doesn't just rely on one person. I often bring in many other experts and collaborate with them.

"As far as making a career of this, I think the best route to go would be investigating phenomena, then turning your material into articles. Be a writer specializing in this area. That's where you could get the income. But I do have to caution that if you are really interested in being a freelance writer and making a buck, you need to be on the other side of the belief coin. You can sell a pro-ghost story far easier than you can sell one that debunks it.

"But if truth and honesty matter to you, you will not sell out. You will report fairly and thoroughly."

Training for Parapsychologists and Paranormal Investigators

There are very few university programs in this country now devoted to training parapsychologists or their counterpart debunkers. The sixties and seventies saw a surge of popularity in these areas, but most have now gone by the wayside. Readers will have to utilize their finely tuned sleuthing skills to track down existing programs. Three leads have been given to you in the appendix: the Institute for Parapsychology, the American Society for Psychical Research (both mostly for believers), and the Center for Inquiry (mostly for nonbelievers).

Joe Nickell offers seminars and workshops under the auspices of the Center for Inquiry. The programs cover investigative techniques, magic used by mind readers and mentalists—and how to detect them—as well as classes on miracles and other interesting phenomena.

Further Reading

Gordon, H. *Extrasensory Deception*. (1988)
Hines, T. *Pseudoscience and the Paranormal*. (1988)
Center for Inquiry. *The Skeptical Inquirer*. P.O. Box 703, Amherst, NY 14226

You may also be interested in the following books written by Joe Nickell:

Inquest on the Shroud of Turin. Prometheus Books
Secrets of the Supernatural. Prometheus Books
Entities. Prometheus Books
Looking for a Miracle. Prometheus Books
Pen Ink, and Evidence. University of Kentucky Press
Ambrose Bierce Is Missing. University of Kentucky Press
Camera Clues. University of Kentucky Press
Detecting Forgery. University of Kentucky Press

Mysteries from the Past

S ome mystery buffs work as diggers, both literally and figuratively—they dig for information about the past. Some dig through mounds of dirt for relics and other evidence of past civilizations and cultures; others seek facts digging through mounds of paper.

Historians

The term *historian* covers a large range of career options and job settings. In general historians study, assess, and interpret the past to determine what happened and why. They examine court documents, diaries, letters, and newspaper accounts: they interview individuals and study archaeological and artifactual evidence. They conduct research, write, teach, evaluate, and make recommendations.

Historians work in schools and universities, in libraries and museums, in government offices and private enterprises.

Under the general term of *historian* come many varied career paths. This chapter examines the following job titles: archaeologist, landscape archaeologist, genealogist, archivist, and researcher.

The Profession of Archaeology

Archaeology is a subdivision of the field of anthropology. Archaeologists study the artifacts of past cultures to learn about their history, customs, and living habits. They survey and excavate archaeological sites, recording and cataloging their finds. By careful analysis archaeologists reconstruct earlier cultures and determine their influence on the present.

Archaeological sites are the physical remains of past civilizations. They can include building debris and the items found inside, even trash and garbage. Usually these sites have been buried by other, later human activity or by natural processes.

Excavation of these sites is a painstaking process conducted by professionals using modern techniques. Because these sites are so fragile, the very nature of excavating destroys some information. With this in mind, archaeologists are careful to dig only as much as they need to answer important questions. Frequently archaeologists concentrate their work on sites slated to be destroyed for highways or new building construction.

Job Settings for Archaeologists

Archaeologists work in a variety of settings. The following chart lists these settings and the duties specific to each.

Archaeologists conducting field work often work with several other professionals in a team effort. They are assisted by geologists, ethnologists, educators, anthropologists, ecologists, and aerial photographers.

In the field archaeologists use a variety of tools during an excavation. These include picks, shovels, trowels, wheelbarrows, sifting boxes, pressure sprayers, and brushes. Archaeologists also make drawings and sketches on site and take notes and photographs.

What It Takes to Become an Archaeologist

Do you have what it takes to become an archaeologist? Take this self-evaluation quiz and find out.

Setting	Duties	Working Conditions
Universities and colleges, Private institutions	Teaching, Field work, Research, Directing student field work	Classroom, Labs, Office space
Museums	Field work, Research, Classifying, Preserving, Displaying	Display and research areas, office space
Public sector (local, state, and national government agencies)	Excavating, Surveying, Analyzing, Preserving, Recording	Sites, Labs, Research facilities
Private sector (construction companies, architectural firms)	Excavating, Surveying, Preserving, Recording	Sites, Labs, Research facilities

Put a check mark under the appropriate heading.   YES   NO

I have above average academic ability.   ____   ____

I have an avid interest in science and history.   ____   ____

Hours of strenuous activity (lifting, carrying, shoveling) do not pose a problem for me.   ____   ____

I have been told I have leadership qualities.   ____   ____

The idea of continuing study throughout my career appeals to me.   ____   ____

I am a logical and analytic thinker.   ____   ____

I enjoy working independently.   ____ ____

I function well as part of a team.   ____ ____

I believe professional ethics should be strictly
adhered to.   ____ ____

I can live under primitive conditions in remote
areas.   ____ ____

To consider yourself a potential archaeologist, you must have
been able to check YES for every question. Even with just one NO
you might want to reconsider your choice of field. Archaeology is
an extremely rigorous and competitive profession.

The Preparation You'll Need

To qualify as a professional archaeologist, graduate study leading to
a master's degree is necessary. A doctoral degree is often preferable.
Most graduate programs in archaeology are found in anthropoloagy
departments. There are about thirty or so universities maintaining
schools of archaeology; these can be found listed in *Peterson's Guide
to Graduate and Professional Programs* (see end of this chapter). To
gain the necessary background on the undergraduate level, a study
of anthropology, history, art, geology, or a related field should be
pursued. At the graduate level students following a course in archaeology would also have to include cultural and physical anthropology, and linguistics in their curriculum.

Where the Jobs Are

Relatively few openings exist in the field of teaching archaeology.
Recently, however, more federal grants and contracts have been
made available for archaeological field work and research. A lot of
this work is being conducted in western and southwestern states
such as Colorado, Arizona, and New Mexico. Particularly in north-
western New Mexico there is a strong industry developing resources
such as gas and oil. Because much of the land there is owned by

the Bureau of Land Management, they have to hire professional archaeologists to clear the site before gas lines or wells can be put in.

In addition to that, the building of a reservoir on the Dolores River in Colorado uncovered hundreds of archaeological sites, necessitating a great deal of archaeological work. The project, which is the largest on the continent and has a very generous budget, has since brought many archaeologists to that area.

Interested mystery buffs who do not desire a full-time professional career as an archaeologist but would like to experience archaeological work can find many opportunities to try their hands at a dig. If you are willing to invest your time, and in some cases your money, you can easily find professionally supervised archaeological investigations taking on volunteers. These are listed in *Archaeology* magazine or in the books mentioned at the end of this chapter. A few examples are provided here:

Crow Canyon Archaeological Center
23390, County Road K
Cortez, CO 81321

University Research
Expeditions Program
Department J-4
University of California
Berkeley, CA 94720

The Smithsonian Institution
Smithsonian National Associates
Research Expedition Program
490 L'Enfant Plaza, SW
Suite 4210
Washington, DC 20560

Earthwatch
680 Maunt Auburn Street
Box 403N
Watertown, MA 02272

Center for American Archeology
Department B
Kampsville Archeological Center
P.O. Box 366
Kampsville, IL 62053

Foundations for Field Research
P.O. Box 2010
Alpine, CA 91001

Crow Canyon Archaeological Center

Crow Canyon is a nonprofit research and educational institution funded by tuition fees, donations, and federal grants. They have an eight-acre campus in southwestern Colorado near Mesa Verde National Park, with a staff of fifty or so archaeologists, educators, and support personnel. In addition to their own research, they instruct participants, both adults and children, who want to learn about archaeology. From junior high age on, participants are taken into the field and taught excavation, recording, and documentation techniques. They also work in the lab a few days a week, learning analysis techniques and methods for cleaning artifacts.

Children too young to work in the field can still participate in a simulated dig in a lab Crow Canyon has set up for that purpose. There they can learn the same excavating techniques as they sift through large, shallow sandboxes where artifacts and walls and other features are buried, just as they would be in the field.

Participants come from all over the United States on educational vacations and stay for a three- to five-day program. Crow Canyon also works with about a dozen graduate students of archaeology a year, providing rewarding internships.

During the summer months participants sleep in cabin tents or in *hogans*, circular Navaho-style structures.

In Montezuma County, where Crow Canyon is located, there are over 10,000 archaeological sites. Crow Canyon professionals at the time this book was written were working at two different nearby sites—Sand Canyon Pueblo and Castle Rock Pueblo, both on Bureau of Land Mangement land. The sites were once Anasazi Indian villages. The Anasazi are the ancestors of present-day Pueblo Indians and were in this area of Colorado from the sixth century until about the year 1300. When they vacated the area, they headed for various points south and relocated. The Crow Canyon team's research is focusing on solving the mystery of when exactly the Anasazi left and why. They are also investigating the political and social systems of the Anasazi.

An Archaeologist at Crow Canyon

Kristin Kuckelman is a field archaeologist at Crow Canyon Archaeologist Center. Her curiosity about the field began when she was a child. Kristin's father was in the Air Force, and she traveled with her parents around the world. They were interested in different cultures and in archaeology and passed that interest on to their daughter. When it came time to go to college, Kristin was naturally drawn to the anthropology program.

Kristin talks about her job:

"I love the variety of it: I enjoy working outdoors, I enjoy writing. And with any kind of research, there's the excitement of discovery. You're trying to solve problems, you're trying to find things out, you're trying to learn something new. And basically every time you go in the field, you hope you're going to learn something about a culture that no one knew before. You don't know what that's going to be; you never really know how it's going to turn out or what you're going to find.

"The sites in this particular area are very easy to discern. They have many hundreds of masonry rooms with, even after centuries, telltale piles of rubble and thousands of artifacts scattered about the ground. Just from walking around the modern ground surface, you can see the tops of the walls and the depressions in the ground indicating the subterranean chambers.

"Sand Canyon covers about four acres; Castle Rock is smaller, close to three acres, and is situated around the base of a butte, a small flat-topped mountain.

"Because of the subterranean chambers we sometimes have to dig down to $2\frac{1}{2}$ to 3 meters to find the actual floor of the structure. The surface rooms are shallower, but we can still have a meter, a meter and a half filled in.

"We've found lithic artifacts—which are artifacts made out of stone—such as spear and arrow points, and sandstone tools for grinding grain. We've also found tens of thousands of pottery fragments—very rarely do we find a piece that is still intact. And very rarely do we engage in refitting, trying to piece the shards together. With so many pieces scattered over the ground, it would take many years, be very, very expensive, and would certainly drive someone crazy!

"Beginning with the first week in May, which is the start of our field season, my partner and I head out to the site, set up equipment, and make sure we have the areas we want excavated all laid out and prepared. We take care of all our paperwork and any mapping we have to do so we're ready for participants to begin digging. During the digging season, we take participants out two or three days a week, but the first full day is spent on campus. Our educators give them a full orientation about archaeology in general. Out in the field, we give them a site tour to give them a background on what it is we're going to be digging, why we're digging, what we're trying to learn. We then give them tools and individual instruction and place them, either individually or in pairs, at the particular places we want excavated.

"Basically we move dirt and put it in a bucket and then take it to a screening station, which is a quarter-inch mesh screen. The dirt gets sifted through the screen to make sure we're not losing any artifacts. Everybody has their own bag, to keep artifacts from each excavation area separate.

"Near the end of the season, we have quite a bit of documentation and mapping to do, and we wash and analyze the artifacts. When we're finished with them, most of the artifacts are put in storage, though a few are rotated as exhibits at the Anasazi Heritage Center, a federally run curation facility.

"Then we have to fill the areas we've dug back in with all the screened dirt and rocks we originally dug out. The idea is, if you were to walk across the site a year later, you'd never know there had been an excavation there. For safety reasons we can't leave gaping holes in the land, and in terms of conservation, to leave a pit open to the elements would damage the site. Before we close it back up, we line the pit with landscaping fabric to protect it and to provide a clue in case future archaeologists are digging there but do not have access to our notes and maps. The lining would show them the site had already been excavated. There are so many sites, and to keep a site open and developed for public exhibit, as has been done at Mesa Verde, would be extremely expensive. It would also be very hard on the architecture itself. Constant maintenance would have to be performed, or everything would eventually deteriorate.

"During the winter we write up in report form everything we learned the previous summer. We also write articles for professional journals and present papers at archaeological conferences across the country."

Kristin's Background

Kristin graduated in 1975 with a B.A. in anthropology and psychology from Colorado Women's College (which has now merged with the University of Denver) and earned her master's degree in anthropology with a concentration in archaeology from the University of Texas at Austin in 1977.

Landscape Archaeology

"There is a new discipline called landscape archeology," Kent Brinkley explains. "The purpose is to recover enough evidence to recreate a garden that existed on the site in a given historical period. Landscape archaeology uses traditional archaeological techniques to recover the fence lines, planting beds, and other evidence."

Kent Brinkley is a landscape architect and garden historian at Colonial Williamsburg. He has been with the foundation for more than ten years.

Kent talks about his job:

"I wear a lot of different hats. I sit at a drawing board and I do designs for new work that's taking place. We also have lots of gardens that were designed during the 1930s and '40s by my predecessors, Arthur Shurcliff and Alden Hopkins. They did a lot of research and picked plants that were known and used in the eighteenth century. But in a few cases a plant they chose, even though it was appropriate to the period, might not have been happy in a specific location because of too much sunlight or too much shade. So we try to come up with something else that would have been used but will grow better and flourish in that specific location.

"Many of these gardens are getting on in years. They're forty or fifty years old, and unlike the architecture where you just replace fabric when a board rots or you're putting a coat of paint on, plant materials do grow. They're dynamic, and when you have a garden that's mature—or overmature, as many of ours happen to be—part of my charge is looking at the replacements that inevitably have to be factored in when plants or trees die out. This keeps it looking presentable to the public.

"I work closely with the person who is responsible for the maintenance. I provide the design expertise, and we talk about what is needed in a particular garden. Once a decision has been made, he directs his maintenance staff to implement the work.

"I'm also a garden historian. That is someone who has a background in history and has done research and is interested in the development of the historical landscape over time. I've made any number of trips to England in the last fourteen or fifteen years and have visited many country estates and gardens over there. I've looked at English landscape design, which served as the precedent for many of the designs in the eighteenth century here in the Virginia Colony. Much of my work involves looking at what was done historically in gardens. The kinds of plants that were grown, how they were laid out, the types of fencing they were using—it's all part of knowing how to recreate a period garden.

"It's a specialty someone comes to within a history curriculum. It's a young field in this country: it didn't start as a discipline until 1975.

"Part of my job is to work in concert with archaeologists when they're doing excavations on a particular site. Right now a summer field school from the College of William and Mary is going on, and we're excavating a garden in town. I'm interested in what they'll find there because this particular site was the home of Saint George Tucker, a fairly prominent Virginian in the eighteenth century whose papers have survived. We know a good bit about his interest in gardening and the things he was growing, so we're all very curious to see what the archaeology will turn up, if we find any physical evidence of his garden. We're digging in the spot where the original garden was. We expect to find evidence of pathways, fence lines, and post holes—they leave a definite dark stain. We can also find planting beds and outbuilding foundations—brick foundations of dairies and chicken coops.

"When you excavate the soil from the planting bed, you sometimes find seed materials in the soil samples. You screen the soil and take it into a lab. There's a method known as flotation that separates the water from the soil, and any minute particles, seeds, and things can be recovered. Then using a microscope, you can identify the type of plant from the seed. We can also do pollen analysis. But it's problematical because you don't always know how the seeds ended up in the bed. They could have been dropped by birds or blown by wind.

"But with *phytolith analysis* we can solve that problem. Phytolith analysis looks at the mineralized tissues of plants. A plant absorbs water and minerals through its root system. When a plant dies, the liquid material will crystallize, and when it does, it takes on an impression of the plant-cell wall structure. Then all the phytoliths are deposited in the soil as the plant decays. So unlike seeds or pollen, which could have gotten there for a number of reasons, when you find phytolith in the soil sample, you can be 99 percent certain the plant was actually grown there and didn't just happen."

Kent's Background

Kent Brinkley has a B.A. in history from Mary Baldwin College in Staunton, Virginia. "I'm a dying breed—you see it less and less. But I came to landscape architecture through the back door. Just as lawyers used to be able to read the law under a licensed practitioner and then sit for the bar exam, years ago you used to be able to apprentice in a landscape architecture office under a licensed practitioner. It was an equal-time commitment. In other words, when you got a five-year B.L.A. degree, you generally had to work in an office three years before you could sit for the exam. Or in lieu of that, you could do eight years in an office and then take the exam. I waited ten years before I took the exam.

"I started as a draftsman and worked my way up to vice president of the firm before coming to Williamsburg.

"When I got my job at Williamsburg, I was ecstatic. This was the perfect marriage of my love of history and my work as a landscape architect. It's been wonderful to be able to take two major interests and combine them in a way that allows you to do both."

How to Get Started

Just as with gardening history, there is no particular university degree at this time in landscape archaeology. To become a landscape archaeologist, you would have to follow a traditional program in anthropology and archaeology. Then once you graduated and started getting on-the-job experience, you could specialize.

If this field interests you, you would combine history courses with horticulture courses. Of course, the job market is fairly small. But it is growing. Right now most jobs are at living history museums such as Williamsburg, or Sturbridge Village and Plimoth Plantation in Massachusetts.

Genealogy

The study of *genealogy*, tracing family histories, has recently become one of the most popular hobbies in the United States. Almost everyone has a keen interest in his or her family background. Genealogists interview older family members; visit courthouses, cemeteries, and libraries, and spend hours poring through diaries, old newspaper accounts, marriage licenses, and birth and death certificates.

Many genealogy hobbyists take their interest one step further and become self-employed genealogists. helping others to dig up their family trees. Genealogists also are employed in historical societies and libraries with special genealogy rooms. The Church of Jesus Christ of Latter-day Saints in Salt Lake City, for example, has a huge repository of family information in a subterranean library. They employ genealogists all over the world or include genealogists who have been accredited through their own program on a list of freelance researchers. For more information write:

Accreditation Program
Family History Library
35 North West Temple Street
Salt Lake City, UT 84150

Other genealogists find work teaching their skills to others in adult education classes, editing genealogy magazines, or writing books or newspaper genealogy columns.

Most genealogists are not formally trained, though specializing in genealogy is possible through some university history and library science programs. In addition, a genealogist can become board-certified. For information on certification requirements and procedures, write to:

Board for Certification of Genealogists
P.O. Box 5816
Falmouth, VA 22403-5816

Salaries for Genealogists

Salaries vary depending upon the institution where a genealogist is employed and upon the level of expertise he or she has reached. Self-employed genealogists make anywhere from fifteen to thirty-five dollars an hour.

How to Get Started

The National Genealogical Society makes the following suggestions for beginners:

QUESTION OLDER FAMILY MEMBERS   Encourage them to talk about their childhoods and relatives, and listen carefully for clues they might inadvertently drop. Learn good interviewing techniques so you ask questions that elicit the most productive answers. Use a tape recorder, and try to verify each fact through a separate source.

VISIT YOUR LOCAL LIBRARY   Become familiar with historical and genealogical publications (a few sources are provided at the end of this chapter), and contact local historical societies. Check out the state library and the archives in your state capital. Seek out any specialty ethnic or religious libraries, and visit cemeteries.

VISIT COURTHOUSES   Cultivate friendships with busy court clerks. Ask to see source records, such as wills, deeds, marriage books, and birth and death certificates.

ENTER INTO CORRESPONDENCE   Write to other individuals or societies involved with the same families or regions. Contact foreign embassies in Washington, D.C. Restrict yourself to asking only one question in each letter you send. Include the information you have already uncovered. Include a self-addressed stamped envelope to encourage replies.

BECOME COMPUTER LITERATE   Members of the National Genealogical Society can participate in a special computer interest section. It encourages the use of computers in research, record management, and data sharing.

KEEP PAINSTAKING RECORDS   Use printed family group sheets or pedigree charts. Develop a well-organized filing system so you'll be able to easily find your information. Keep separate records for each family you research.

WRITE THE NATIONAL GENEALOGICAL SOCIETY   Take advantage of their forty-six–page book, *Beginners in Genealogy*, their charts, and their library loan program. You can also enroll in their home study course called "American Genealogy: A Basic Course." Their address is listed in the appendix.

Archivists

Nobody knows the exact number, but it's estimated that there are close to 5000 archives in the United States. Each of the fifty states maintains a government archive, as do most city and county governments. Archives will also be found in universities, historical societies, museums, libraries, and private businesses.

On the national level there is the National Archives in Washington, D.C., which looks after the records of the federal government. The Library of Congress provides information services to the U.S. Congress and technical services to all the libraries across the country.

What Are Archives?

Although archives are similar to libraries. there are distinct differences between the two. Libraries typically house materials that are published and were created with the express purpose of broad dissemination. Archives typically hold materials that were created in the course of some business or activity but were never intended originally for public dissemination. For example, in an archive you might find letters from a Civil War soldier to his family. He wrote about his experiences and feelings and to let his loved ones know that he was still alive, surviving this or that battle. He never would have imagined that his correspondence would one day appear in an archive. This gives his letters credibility, an integrity as a historical source. The newspaper reporter covering the same battles wrote with a specific point of view for widespread publication, ultimately for the purpose of selling newspapers.

Archives handle collections that chart the course of daily life for individuals and businesses. Some archives specifically look after materials created by their own institution. Coca-Cola Co., for example, set up an archive years ago to have a history of what the company business was and how it prospered. New companies set up archives to keep a documented record.

Educational institutions such as universities or museums create archives that relate to their special research interests.

The material found in an archive can include letters, personal papers, and organizational records. Archives created within the last 100 years or so can also contain visual records, such as photographs, postcards, prints, drawings, and sketches. Today archives also collect phonograph records, audiotapes, videotapes, movie films and computer-stored information.

Who Uses Archives?

Because archives hold firsthand information, they are valuable to anyone with an interest in the people, places, and events of the past. This group includes genealogists, museum researchers, scholars and students, writers, and historians.

What Does an Archivist Do?

As with libraries and archives, there are distinct differences between librarians and archivists, including the way they operate and the methods and techniques they use to handle material.

The one biggest difference is that librarians look at materials they get on an item-by-item basis. Each book is a distinct entity evaluated separately from the other books. In an archive a single letter would usually be part of a larger collection of letters. Archivists are interested in these as a group because one letter would only be a fragment. To really understand something about the past, the information needs to be synthesized and put together in a collection.

When archivists talk about their work, they discuss certain basic functions that are common to all archives. The numbers following the five areas below designate the percentage of time usually spent with each duty.

Arrangement and description of collections	60%
Identification and acquisition of materials	10%
Preservation of collections	10%
Reference services	15%
Community outreach and public affairs	5%

John Fleckner, Chief Archivist at the Smithsonian Institution's National Museum of American History

John Fleckner came to the Smithsonian in 1982 with more than a decade's experience working as an archivist for the State Historical Society of Wisconsin. He is a past president of the Society of American Archivists and has acted as a consultant on many important archives projects, including the United Negro College Fund, the Viet Nam History and Archives Project, and the Native American Archives Project.

John did his undergraduate work at Colgate, in Hamilton, New York, graduating in 1963 with a B.A. with honors in history. He earned his master's degree in American history at the University of Wisconsin in 1965. He has also completed much of the work required for earning a Ph.D.

The archive John is responsible for acquires collections from the outside and does not handle the records generated by the museum. Their collections cover a wide range of subjects and are particularly strong in the areas of American music, advertising, and the history of technology.

At the Smithsonian John oversees a professional staff of twelve archivists, three student interns, and close to twenty volunteers.

John talks about how he became an archivist:

"After too many years of graduate school, pursuing a vague notion of teaching college-level history, I realized that I really didn't want to teach. I was so naive it took a university career counselor to recognize that my history background might be anything other than an economic liability. Leaning back in her chair, she pointed out her office window to the State Historical Society of Wisconsin just across the street, and she directed me to a recently established graduate program in archives administration. The instructor would make no promises about the prospects for a job, but with a sly smile he offered that all his previous students were working. I didn't need a weatherman—as they said in those days, the early 1970s—to tell me which way the wind was blowing.

"So it was an accident in good guidance that got me in the door. But it was the experience of doing archival work—beginning with the simplest class exercises and then a formal internship—that sealed it for me. I loved the combination of handicraft and analytical work, and I loved the intense, intimate contact with the 'stuff' of history. Before I completed my internship, I knew I wanted to be an archivist.

"Previously as a graduate student, of course I had done some research in archives—at the Library of Congress, the College of William and Mary, and especially the State Historical Society. But the archivists had taken all the fun out of it—the materials were antiseptically foldered, boxed, and listed.

"Wheeled out on carts, they were like cadavers to be dissected by first-year medical students. On occasion I even donned white gloves. The documents always seemed lifeless.

"Later as a would-be archivist, they thrilled me. I was in charge; I would evaluate their significance, determine their order, describe their contents, and physically prepare them for their permanent resting places. Still, it was not so much this heady feeling of control that awed me but more the mystery, the possibilities of the records themselves.

"My judgments would be critical to building paths to the records for generations of researchers, across the entire spectrum of topics, and into unknown future time.

"The archival enterprise held another attractive feature for me. For all the opportunity to reconstruct the past captured in these documents and to imagine the future research they might support, I had a well-defined task to accomplish, a product to produce, techniques and methods for proceeding, and standards against which my work would be judged. There was rigor and discipline; this was real work. And as good fortune would have it, I soon was getting paid to do it."

How You Can Become an Archivist

People get into the archives profession in a variety of traditional and unusual ways. Often in a small town, an archives is a closet in the back room of a local historical society's office. Someone volunteers to put it all together, perhaps the oldest person in the community with a strong interest in the area's history.

The standard way to become an archivist is to have an undergraduate degree with a history background, and a graduate degree, at least at the master's level, that would involve specific course work in archives. There are thirty to fifty programs, which are often in graduate library schools. The Society of American Archivists publishes a directory of these educational programs.

Many archivists have a Master of Library Science (M.L.S.) degree with a concentration in archives, but sometimes archives courses are also taught in history departments.

Salaries for Archivists

Archivists with a master's degree can expect to start out in the mid- to high twenties. Someone with ten years' experience as an archivist with administrative responsibilities for the Smithsonian might earn $60,000 a year or more.

Researchers in a Living History Museum

Researchers can find work in a variety of settings: university archaeology and history departments, preservation boards, libraries and archives, and government offices.

Carolyn Trewers, director of research at Plimoth Plantation, works in an unconventional place: a living history museum. Researchers are the backbone behind every living history museum. Without their efforts accurately recreating authentic period characters, restoring historic buildings, or reproducing a facsimile of daily life would be an impossible task.

Carolyn talks about her job:

"We have four sites at Plimoth Plantation: the 1627 Pilgrim village; the *Mayflower II*; Hobbamock's Homesite, a Wampanohg Indian; and the Carriage House Crafts Center. We research anything we need for our program, from what is the period attitude toward toads, how a character felt about being her husband's third wife, or the correct way to cook a particular dish to some obscure point of Calvinist theology. The women are more difficult to research than the men because there is less documented information on them. You are forced into recreating a more typical persona than the actual character; sort of a generic portrayal. In general we research the life and genealogical background and social history for all the characters we portray.

"In our research we use a variety of sources—court records and genealogical research done by professional genealogists such as the General Society of Mayflower Descendants or writers for the *American Genealogist* or other genealogy periodicals.

"We also have researchers in other departments. For example, the authenticity of buildings and structures is done more by our curatorial department."

Carolyn's Background

Carolyn attended Earlham College, a small Quaker school in Richmond, Indiana, where she earned a B.A. in fine arts with a concentration in history. She then went on to Simmons Graduate School of Library and Information Science in Boston and graduated in 1981 with master's in library and information science, with a concentration in research methods.

Carolyn grew up in Plymouth and started work at the age of fourteen as a part-time Pilgrim. After she finished her master's degree, she returned to Plimoth Plantation as a researcher.

The Qualifications You'll Need

Carolyn points out that researching is a competitive field and that a higher degree, in history or library science with a research methods concentration, is necessary.

A candidate is not expected to have a general body of knowledge about the specific time period, but he or she must have strong research skills, talent, and experience.

Salaries for Researchers

New graduates might begin with a salary as low as the mid-teens. "You don't do it for the money," Carolyn stresses. "There are a lot of psychological payments. One of the satisfactions is to be able to change someone's mind about the stereotypes surrounding early colonists."

Further Reading
General

Peterson's Guide to Graduate and Professional Programs. Princeton, N.J.: Peterson's. Annual.

Chronicle Guidance Publications. Briefs explaining these professions: anthropologists, archaeologists, criminologists, demographers, economists, genealogists, geographers, librarians, linguists, museum curators, political scientists, sociologists. Aurora Street, P.O. Box 1190, Moravia, NY 13118-1190.

Archaeology

Archaeological Institute of America. *Archaeological Fieldwork Opportunities Bulletin.* Kendall Hunt Publishing Company, Order Department, 2640 Kerper Boulevard, Dubuque, IA 52001. (800) 338-5578. It is a comprehensive guide to excavations, field schools, and special programs throughout the world with openings for volunteers, students, staff, and technicians.

American Anthropological Association. *Summer Field School List.* 1703 New Hampshire Avenue, NW, Washington, D.C. 20009, (202) 232-8800.

National Park Service. *LEAP: Listing of Education in Archeological Programs.* P.O. Box 37127, Washington, D.C. 20013-7127. Attn: LEAP coordinator, DCA/ADD.

Elting, Franklin, and Mary Elting. *America's Ancient Treasures.* University of New Mexico Press.

Renfrew, Colin, and Paul Bahn, *Archeology: Theories, Methods, and Practice.* New York: Thames and Hudson.

Fagan, Brian. *The Adventure of Archeology.* Washington, D.C.: National Geographic Society.

Magazines

Archaeology (bimonthly)
National Geographic (monthly)
Scientific American (monthly)
Smithsonian (monthly)

Professional Journals

These journals, though not available in every local library, can be found in university libraries or in large public libraries.

American Antiquity
Historical Archaeology
Journal of Anthropological Archaeology
Journal of Field Archaeology
North American Archaeologist

CHAPTER SEVEN

Mysteries of Science

A mystery buff could get lost in this vast area of career possibilities that use research and investigative skills.

The field of science covers everything from the human mind to animal behavior, to medical research, to the far-off planets in the universe. It would take an encyclopedia to cover all the choices. So in true detective style, the best suggestion is for you to use this chapter as a starting-off point. Once you've narrowed the field, you'll have to continue your research, digging up more information on the various careers. Some resources have been listed for you at the end of this chapter and in the appendix.

Mysteries of the Mind

Many mystery buffs are intrigued by the human mind. What makes us tick? How do we learn? What motivates us? What causes us to react, think, and feel the way we do?

Psychology

As a mystery buff you might have read Jonathan Kellerman's books featuring the hero Alex Delaware. He's a child psychologist who inevitably gets involved playing the role of detective as well as doctor for his troubled patients.

Most psychologists don't get involved in police matters (unless they are working for or with the police). But they do conduct a special kind of detective work, probing the human psyche, trying to understand the human condition in order to offer help to individuals and groups.

Psychologists study human behavior and mental processes to understand, explain, and change people's behavior. They may study the way a person thinks, feels, or behaves. Research psychologists inverstigate the physical, cognitive, emotional, and social aspects of human behavior. Psychologists in applied fields counsel and conduct training programs; do market research; apply psychological treatments to a variety of medical and surgical conditions; and provide mental health services in hospitals, clinics, and private settings.

Like other social scientists, psychologists formulate hypotheses and collect data to test the hypotheses' validity. Research methods depend on the topic under study. Psychologists may gather information through controlled laboratory experiments; personality, performance, aptitude, or intelligence tests; observation, interviews, or questionnaires; clinical studies; or surveys. Computers are widely used to record and analyze this information.

Psychology Specialties

In addition to the variety of work settings, psychologists specialize in many different areas.

Clinical Psychologists, who constitute the largest specialty, generally work in independent or group practice or in hospitals or clinics. They may help the mentally or emotionally disturbed adjust to life and are increasingly helping all kinds of medical and surgical patients deal with their illnesses or injuries. They may work in physical medicine and rehabilitation settings, treating patients with spinal cord injuries; chronic pain or illness; stroke; and arthritis and neurological conditions, such as multiple sclerosis. Others help people deal with life stresses such as divorce or aging.

Clinical psychologists interview patients; give diagnostic tests; provide individual, family, and group psychotherapy; and design and implement behavior modification programs. They may collaborate with physicians and other specialists in developing treatment programs and help patients understand and comply with the prescribed treatment.

Some clinical psychologists work in universities, where they train graduate students in the delivery of mental health and behavioral medicine services. Others administer community mental health programs. Counseling psychologists use several techniques, including interviewing and testing, to advise people on how to deal with problems of everyday living, whether personal, social, educational, or vocational.

DEVELOPMENTAL PSYCHOLOGISTS study the patterns and causes of behavioral change as people progress through life from infancy to adulthood. Some concern themselves with behavior during infancy, childhood, and adolescence, whereas others study changes that take place during maturity and old age. The study of developmental disabilities and how they affect people is a new area within developmental psychology.

EDUCATIONAL PSYCHOLOGISTS evaluate student and teacher needs and design and develop programs to enhance the educational setting.

EXPERIMENTAL PSYCHOLOGISTS study behavior processes and work with human beings and with animals such as rats, monkeys, and pigeons. Prominent areas of experimental research include motivation, thinking, attention, learning and retention, sensory and perceptual processes, effects of substance use and abuse, and genetic and neurological factors in behavior.

INDUSTRIAL AND ORGANIZATIONAL PSYCHOLOGISTS apply psychological techniques to personnel administration, management, and marketing problems. They are involved in policy planning, applicant screening, training and development, psychological test research, counseling, and organizational development and analysis. For example, an industrial psychologist may work with management to develop better training programs and to reorganize the work setting to improve worker productivity or quality of work life.

SCHOOL PSYCHOLOGISTS work with students, teachers, parents, and administrators to resolve students' problems.

SOCIAL PSYCHOLOGISTS examine people's interactions with others and with the social environment. Prominent areas of study include group behavior, leadership, attitudes, and interpersonal perception. Some relatively new specialties include cognitive psychology, health psychology, neuropsychology, and geropsychology.

COGNITIVE PSYCHOLOGISTS deal with the brain's role in memory, thinking, and perceptions. Some cognitive psychologists do research related to computer programming and artificial intelligence.

HEALTH PSYCHOLOGISTS promote good health through health maintenance counseling programs. Programs might be designed, for example, to help people stop smoking or lose weight.

NEUROPSYCHOLOGISTS study the relation between the brain and behavior. They often work in stroke and head injury programs.

GEROPSYCHOLOGISTS deal with the special problems faced by the elderly. The emergence and growth of these specialties reflects the increasing participation of psychologists in providing direct services to special patient populations.

Other areas of specialization include psychometrics; psychology and the arts; the history of psychology; psychopharmacology; and community, comparative, consumer, engineering, environmental, family, forensic, population, military, and rehabilitation psychology.

Sociology

Those in the know postulate that while psychologists really enter the field to understand and change themselves, sociologists want to be able to take on and change the world around them.

Sociologists study human society and social behavior by examining the groups and social institutions that people form: families, communities, and governments, as well as various social, religious, political, and business organizations. They also study the behavior and interaction of groups, trace their origin and growth, and analyze the influence of group activities on individual members. They are concerned with the characteristics of social groups, organizations, and institutions; the ways individuals are affected by each other and by the groups to which they belong; and the impact of social traits such as gender, age, and race on a person's daily life.

Sociology Specialties

As a rule sociologists work in one or more specialties, such as social organization, stratification, and mobility; revolution, war, and peace; racial and ethnic relations; education; the family; social psychology; urban, rural, political, and comparative sociology: gender roles and relations: and sociological practice. Other specialties include medical sociology, the study of social factors that effect mental and public health; gerontology, the study of aging and the special problems of aged persons; environmental sociology, the study of the effects of the physical environment and technology on people; clinical sociology therapy, analysis, and intervention for individuals, groups, organizations, and communities; demography, the study of the size, characteristics, and movement of populations; criminology, the study of factors producing deviance from accepted legal and cultural norms; and industrial sociology, the study of work and organizations. Other sociologists specialize in research design and data analysis.

Sociologists usually conduct surveys or engage in direct observation to gather data. For example, after providing for controlled conditions, an organizational sociologist might test the effects of different styles of leadership on individuals in a small work group. A medical sociologist might study the effects of terminal illness on family interaction. Sociological researchers also evaluate the efficacy of different kinds of social programs. They might examine and evaluate particular programs of income assistance, job training, health care, or remedial education.

Sociologists extensively use statistical and computer techniques in their research, along with qualitative methods such as focus-group research and social impact assessment.

The results of sociological research aid educators, lawmakers, administrators, and others interested in resolving social problems and formulating public policy. For example, sociologists study issues related to abortion rights, AIDS, high school dropouts, homelessness, and latchkey children. Sociologists often work closely with community groups and members of other professions, including psychologists, physicians, economists, statisticians, urban and regional planners, political scientists, anthropologists, law enforcement and criminal justice officials, and social workers.

Sociologists often are confused with social workers, and in fact both kinds of professionals do contribute to one another's discipline. Whereas most sociologists conduct research on organizations, groups, and individuals, clinical sociologists—like social workers—may directly help people who are unable to cope with their circumstances.

Training for Psychologists and Sociologists

A doctoral degree generally is required for employment as a psychologist. Psychologists with a Ph.D. qualify for a wide range of teaching, research, clinical, and counseling positions in universities, elementary and secondary schools, private industry, and government. Psychologists with a Psy.D. (Doctor of Psychology) degree qualify mainly for clinical positions.

Persons with a master's degree in psychology can administer tests as psychological assistants. Under the supervision of doctoral-level psychologists, they can conduct research in laboratories, conduct psychological evaluations, counsel patients, and perform administrative duties. They may teach in high schools or two-year colleges or work as school psychologists or counselors.

A bachelor's degree in psychology qualifies a person to assist psychologists and other professionals in community mental health centers, vocational rehabilitation offices, and correctional programs; to work as a research or adminstrative assistant; and to take a job as a trainee in government or business. However, without additional academic training, advancement opportunities in psychology are severely limited.

A master's degree in sociology usually is the minimum requirement for employment in applied research or community college teaching. The Ph.D. degree is essential for most senior-level positions in research institutes, consulting firms, corporations, and government agencies and is required for appointment to permanent teaching and research positions in colleges and universities.

Sociologists holding a master's degree can qualify for administrative and research positions in public agencies and private businesses. Training in research, statistical, and computer methods is an advantage in obtaining such positions.

Bachelor's degree holders in sociology often get jobs in related fields. Their training in research, statistics, and human behavior qualifies them for entry-level positions in social services, management, sales, personnel, and marketing. Many work in social service agencies as counselors or child-care, juvenile, or recreation workers. Others are employed as interviewers or as administrative or research assistants. Sociology majors with sufficient training in statistical and survey methods may qualify for positions as junior analysts or statisticians in business or research firms or government agencies. Regardless of a sociologist's level of educational attainment, completion of an internship while in school can prove invaluable in finding a position in sociology or a related field.

Earnings

Salaries vary greatly according to the degree held, the area of specialization, and the geographic area in which the psychologist or sociologist works.

According to a survey by the American Psychological Association, the median annual salary of psychologists with a doctoral degree was $48,000 in counseling psychology, $50,000 in research positions, $53,000 in clinical psychology, $55,000 in school psychology, and $76,000 in industrial/organizational psychology.

In university psychology departments median annual salaries ranged from $32,000 for assistant professors to $55,000 for full professors.

The median annual salary of master's degree holders was $35,000 for faculty, $37,000 in counseling psychology, $40,000 in clinical psychology, $48,000 in research positions, $50,000 in industrial/organizational psychology, and $52,000 in school psychology. Some psychologists, particularly those in private practice, have much higher earnings.

Experienced sociologists with a doctoral degree tend to earn the highest salaries in academia. Those employed in business, industry, and private consulting may earn more than those in academia or in government. The master's degree may be as lucrative as a doctorate in some settings outside of academia.

In general sociologists with the Ph.D. degree earn substantially higher salaries than those with a lesser degree. Some sociologists supplement their regular salaries with earnings from other sources such as consulting, counseling, or writing articles and books. Those who create their own consulting practice find that earnings vary according to how much time they devote to their practice, the type of clients they serve, and the region of the country.

Mysteries of the Universe

If you are content to leave the mysteries of the mind and society to others, then you might be intrigued by all the puzzles the universe has to offer.

There are almost as many job possibilities as there are puzzles. Here's a look at a few career suggestions for working on land, underwater, or in space.

All sorts of scientists study all sorts of aspects of the earth. Look at these questions that need to be answered, then check below to see the different occupations that search for the answers.

On Land

How was our planet formed? Can we predict earthquakes? How can we find oil and other natural resources? How can we best grow crops? How can we save our endangered animals? How can we protect our environment? How can we better plan our cities and roads?

- Geologists
- Engineers
- Environmentalists
- Agricultural scientists
- Ecologists
- Zoologists
- Urban planners
- Developers

Underwater

How were the oceans formed? What natural resources lie below the oceans? What kind of marine life exists in the seas?

- Geologists
- Oceanographers
- Marine biologists

In Space

What are the conditions on other planets and moons? How can we travel more efficiently to distant planets? How can space exploration help us on Earth?

- Engineers
- Astronauts
- Astronomers
- Educators

A Close-up Look at Planetariums

Most of us have visited a planetarium at one time or another and remember the thrill of sitting in a darkened dome, watching the night sky spread above and around us. With a Carl Sagan–type voice explaining the spectacle before us, we witnessed solar and lunar eclipses, the solar corona, comets, auroras, the configuration of the Milky Way, and other astronomical phenomena.

Although many of us were content to view the experience as a form of educational entertainment, a small few—perhaps you who are reading this book—wondered how all the special effects were achieved and how you might make the world of planetariums a part of your future career.

Job Titles within Planetariums

Although the number of employees and job titles varies from planetarium to planetarium, the list below, modeled from the employee roster at the Charles Hayden Planetarium in Boston, contains a representative sample of career positions.

PRODUCERS, who are responsible for tying together all the elements of a show. Media experience and ability in any of the audiovisual multi-image areas is important.

TECHNICIANS, who keep the facility going and make sound tracks or special effects devices such as a rotating galaxy, an exploding meteor, a black hole, or an aurora borealis. People with technical know-how are sought after. You should be able to work with optics and electric and mechanical devices and also be inventive and creative. This field requires practical rather than theoretical knowledge.

PHOTOGRAPHERS, who convert artwork into slide form to incorporate into planetarium shows. Photography training is a must.

ARTISTS, who do graphic arts on the computer or work with an airbrush and various other media. Artists usually learn their technical skills through university art programs.

ASTRONOMERS, who translate research into information accessible to the general public. Those planetariums that are affiliated with universitites or have an observatory would have staff astronomers who are, in addition to teaching and interpreting, involved in research. A master's degree or a Ph.D. is usually required.

EDUCATIONAL PROGRAMMER/COORDINATORS, who develop ideas for shows and research materials for them. A bachelor's degree would be the minimum requirement, but more and more a master's degree is necessary. A background in astronomy would be a plus.

SCRIPTWRITERS, who take the information and research and write the narration part of the show. A scriptwriter could be on staff at a planetarium but also could be a full- or part-time freelancer.

PRESENTERS handle the live portion of the show and interact with the audience. At the Charles Hayden Planetarium almost everybody on the staff takes a turn with running the programs and presenting them.

Larry Schindler, Director of the Charles Hayden Planetarium, Museum of Science, Boston

"The planetarium's job is to portray astronomical and space science phenomena visually and present programs about that. The way it does it is by combining not just a single medium such as a movie, videotape, slide show, star projector, or special effects device, but a combination of those things. It has evolved in such a way that it needs all these different gizmos to show what the people who make the programs want to show on the dome.

"It's not just a single medium, it's a whole bunch of media, and usually it will be under some kind of central control system. Now it's computers; before it used to be manually turning knobs and pushing buttons. There is virtually always a sound track of some sort that goes behind it, like with a movie. The sound track has music and the narration and the sound effects all blended in one continuous string. And then it usually works that the audio track has another data track that then synchronizes the computers that run the whole rest of the show."

It's Done with Mirrors

"The truth of the matter is," Larry confesses, "that a lot of the program is not real stuff—it's fake. When you're trying to create environments, the audience's expectations start to change. A square picture projected onto the dome just doesn't work anymore. If you wanted to show, for example, an image through a telescope and point to a place in the night sky, you could use some kind of photograph. But to be most satisfying, it would need to look like it's floating in midair. This means that you would start off with a slide and then doctor it up so it doesn't have the square format.

"The core of it is a fake night sky that you try to make as real-looking as possible, but you don't do that by taking a picture. For a rotating galaxy you might use some sort of a photograph or artwork and then convert it into the form you need—a transparency you can make go across the dome, or something like that. We use all sorts of materials—pieces of shiny mirrors, and plastic wheels and colored gels."

Mostly the Charles Hayden Planetarium in Boston produces its own shows, but there are also premade packages that can be purchased. "Some of them have been produced under grants," Larry explains, "or some of them are sold by planetariums that produce them. Usually the typical package you get includes a script, a sound track, a bunch of slides or videotape, and then you're on your own to put it all together and make it work in your facility. Every facility is different. It's not that you can take something and just plug it in; it's never that simple."

Who's Running the Show?

Shows are generally under automatic or semiautomatic control. "The one thing the computer doesn't take care of," Larry explains, "is the star projector itself. So even in what you could call a 'canned' program, we need somebody there to turn the right knob at the right time to make the star projector do its thing. But we'll have the capability in a year, though, of automating that too.

"It always requires somebody to run the show. It used to be that the presenter would be at the console, where all the controls are, at one edge of the planetarium—a combination podium and spaceship control board with a microphone, knobs, and buttons. But we are now getting into a presentation method where the person actually goes out in front and walks around in the audience, holding a remote control unit, and conducts the program from out there.

"It takes a lot of different kinds of experience and talents to put this all together. Once you've established the content, it's a lot like producing a film or show."

The Show Is Never Over

So once the show is produced, are all the planetarium's workers out of a job? Larry explains: "There are always more shows to be done and lots of topics to cover. Most planetariums would have a menu of different programs for different age groups, for school groups, for the general public, for families.

"They often take many months to do. Here we have settled in on doing two major public shows a year. We draw on many sources, and they're just multiplying like crazy. We have access to all kinds of NASA material and stuff coming through from the Hubble space telescope, and we incorporate those."

Larry Schindler's Background

Larry earned his B.S. in electrical engineering and humanities from the Massachusetts Institute of Technology. He worked in engineering for a while and started at the planetarium in 1967. His first position was as a lecturer/technician. Half his time he spent fixing and making things, the other half teaching courses and doing the programs, which were mostly live then. He then moved on to become the producer and stayed in that position until he was promoted to director in 1987.

Larry Talks about His Job

"We're a nerve center and contact for information flowing into and out of the planetarium. In the old days it was very possible to make a decision and just do it, like the bumper sticker, but that doesn't hold anymore. Now it involves communicating with three or four other departments, organization meetings. That sort of thing.

"Astronomy is a fascinating subject to begin with. You're dealing with the big picture, and there's a challenge there to try to convey the excitement of it to everybody.

"I'm fascinated with the technology as well. I realize it's just a tool, but to some of the other staff, it's an end in itself. In terms of job satisfaction, the perks you get are to play with all those wonderful toys.

"Sometimes it's pressured, particularly in a large organization where you have a lot of different things to tend to. But I don't think that pressure is a negative. There are odd hours; we're open seven days a week and some nights, but the people who work those hours have a certain amount of choice.

"The downside is nobody is getting rich."

Salaries in Planetariums

Salaries range from institution to institution, but even in the bigger, high-cost cities, salaries are far from glamourous. A producer with experience could expect to earn from $30,000 to $40,000. Artists and photographers earn in the twenties; technicians in the low to high twenties; an astronomer and educational coordinator in the high twenties to low thirties; and the administrative positions, such as director, earn in the thirties to forties.

Some Advice from Larry Schindler

"A background in astronomy isn't absolutely necessary for many of the specific jobs. It can be learned on the job. But you should ask yourself if you've got the interest. Do you like being around and are comfortable with computers and audiovisual equipment?

"I think you also need to be able to deal with the people who attend the programs. Some planetariums are much more teaching-oriented, and they need to deal with students. If you don't like answering people's questions and helping to solve their little problems, you'll probably have a hard time."

Landing That Job

"This is not a huge field," Larry explains, "like the electronics industry is. The key to getting a job in a planetarium is to be in the right place when there's an opening. A lot of times it's the volunteer who has been there regularly who gets the job. They acquire experience through volunteering, and if they show some aptitude and get to know everybody, and if someone leaves and there's an opening, they learn about it."

Planetariums often announce their job openings to other planetariums. Being on-site as a volunteer or intern will put you in a position to know about openings around the country. There is also a job information service for planetariums described later in this chaper.

Noreen Grice, Education Coordinator/ Astronomer, Charles Hayden Planetarium, Museum of Science, Boston

"When I started majoring in astronomy, I was like a lot of other students who weren't really sure what they wanted to do. I just started taking classes. I thought I would end up teaching in a university.

"But what attracted me to this field initially is when I was little we had *Star Trek* and *Lost in Space* on TV, and I found it interesting. I guess I wanted to discover new life forms or learn about where Mr. Spock lived.

"My position is not really a research position. It's more of an educator and liaison between research and the general public. It's a mixed bag. Because I'm the person on staff with an astronomy background, I'm involved in translating the research into information we can present to the public and checking the scientific accuracy of our scripts. I'm also one of the presenters for the shows.

"I'm involved more in the early stages of the production. We have an outside writer for scripts who takes my information to write the script. It is then presented to the producer, who will then distribute it to the rest of the staff to read for how the story flows. But what I look more for is its accuracy, and it usually goes back and forth with the writer.

"I also coordinate special events such as Astronomy Day and Space Week. Astronomy Day is an international event, a day to get some extra interest in astronomy going. I'll contact all the astronomy clubs and the little planetariums in the area and ask them to come and set up a display table, and we'll fill the corridors of the museum with astronomy. We have special shows and at night we'll have a star party, and I'll arrange to have different speakers come in and talk on different topics.

"Space Week is always celebrated from July 16 to July 24. That's more of an aerospace type of focus—NASA and rockets and moon missions.

"I also teach courses. When I came here, the only courses the planetarium offered were a naked-eye astronomy class, a telescopic astronomy class, and two navigation courses, and these were all for adults. The classes were too specialized; they catered only to adults who were interested in boating or buying a telescope. We didn't have any kids' courses, and there were always parents calling up asking for one. So I created courses ranging from preschool all the way up to high school. We cover the Earth and Moon, Sun and stars, the planets of our solar system. One is called 'Galaxies and Other Weird Stuff,' another is 'Astronaut Adventure'.

"I also teach a photography course for adults called 'Star Trails.' People bring their cameras into the planetarium and we turn on the star projector, and they can photograph whatever they want; constellations, the Sun or Moon, or eclipses. We cover the technical aspects of photography.

"I teach two or four hours a week, but the preparation is a lot more. I try to make it very hands-on, and the kids make sundials, constellation viewers, or models of black holes. They can take what they've made home with them.

"I have some administrative duties; organizing the planetarium's show schedule—we could have three to eight shows in one day—keeping tabs on course supplies, that sort of thing.

"I also answer questions from the public and answer letters from school kids, especially around science fair week. I noticed that everyone was asking the some questions. At first I wrote an individual reply to each person, but it was taking a lot of time, so I came up with fifteen brochures on different astronomy topics.

"I'm interested in astronomy and I'm interested in people, and I think it's a good mix here in the planetarium. The downside is that working in a planetarium can isolate you. A lot of research is going on, and I'm not in the midst of it as if I were in an academic setting."

Some Advice from Noreen Grice

"I think it's most important for a person to have a degree in astronomy, especially in this position. [Noreen earned a bachelor's in astronomy from Boston University in 1985 and her master's in astronomy from San Diego State University in 1987.] It would be very difficult to read over material for scientific accuracy without a foundation. It would give you an edge over the competition and peace of mind knowing in your heart that what you're reading is accurate. When we do a show, my name's on the dome, and I don't want to put my seal of approval on anything unless I'm sure.

"Physics, earth science, and education would give you skills in teaching but not interpreting. The way planetariums are set up, you have a group of researchers out there making the discoveries. The person in the planetarium needs to know how to interpret what that research is and understand its relevance."

Further Reading

Lucas, Jerry. *Great Unsolved Mysteries of Science*. F & W Publications. This book for teenagers explores six baffling puzzles.

The Occupational Outlook Handbook. Washington, D.C.: Department of Labor. The OOH, as it is also known, lists about every job imaginable, giving job descriptions, working conditions, training requirements, salary expectations, and job outlook. It is available in the reference section of any public library.

For More Information
Psychology

For information on careers, educational requirements, financial assistance, and licensing in all fields of psychology, contact:

American Psychological Association
Education in Psychology and Accreditation Offices
Education Directorate
750 First Street, NE
Washington, DC 20002

Information about state licensing requirements is available from:

Association of State and Provincial Psychology Boards
P.O. Box 4389
Montgomery, AL 36103

Information on traineeships and fellowships also is available from colleges and universities that have graduate departments of psychology.

Sociology

Additional information on careers, certification, and graduate departments of sociology is available from:

American Sociological Association
1722 N Street, NW
Washington, DC 20036-2981

For information about careers and certification in clinical and applied sociology, contact:

Sociological Practice Association
Department of Pediatrics/Human Development
B240 Life Sciences
Michigan State University
East Lansing, MI 48824-1317

Job Information Service for Planetariums

The International Planetarium Society operates a job information service. To receive notification of new positions opening in the planetarium field, send up to six self-addressed stamped envelopes to:

Donald Hall, Director
Strasenburgh Planetarium
P.O. Box 1480
Rochester, NY 14603

Mystery for Fun and Profit

M any innovative people have combined their love for a good mystery with other talents or acquired skills. With a good imagination a dedicated mystery buff can bring in extra income or create a specialized career. Here are a couple of successful ventures that might spark some ideas of your own.

Mystery Walking Tours

If you're comfortable talking with small groups of people, like to walk, know how to conduct research, and can put together a one- to two-hour presentation, then starting a mystery walking tour might be a fun way to bring in some additional earnings.

Basically the leader of a mystery walking tour escorts a group of (paying) people to designated sites and landmarks in a particular area. At each stop the leader gives a talk on that particular spot, telling about its history or notoriety and answering questions.

Mystery walking tours are usually organized around a particular theme. Stops on the route can cover homes of famous mystery writers or focus on where crimes or scandals occurred. For example, a tour of Boston could follow the killing spree route of the Boston Strangler. Palm Beach, Florida, offers plenty of grist for the gossip mill, and even an island as small as Key West has had its share of titillating incidents.

How far you can go with this idea depends in part on where you live and how active criminals or mystery writers are in your area. Follow these ten steps to get started:

1. Research your area. Visit the public library, check out courthouse records, or ask to be allowed into the newspaper morgue. You're looking for past events or notorious residents, but remember they must all be within walking distance of each other.

2. If your research is fruitful, decide how long a tour you have enough material for. Then organize your information to follow the different stops you'll make. Allow ten minutes or so for each spot. Get as many juicy details as possible. Gory and gruesome details will work well, too. (Remember, everyone loves a good mystery!)

3. Decide on a price. You probably won't get rich doing this, but don't scare off customers with too high an admission ticket. Anywhere from four to seven dollars is a good ballpark figure to charge for each person. You can give discounts for children or senior citizens. The more you have in your group, the more you'll make.

4. How often will you offer the tour? Every Saturday morning? Sunday afternoons? If the area warrants it, you could run one or two a day. It's up to you.

5. Make a dry run. Walk the tour yourself, or take along friends and family. It's unlikely that you'll be able to enter any of the buildings without making some sort of arrangement with owners, so be sure to pick out a spot where you and your group can pause to talk. Under a shady tree is good for summer days, but be careful not to block vehicular or pedestrian traffic.

6. Check with local officials regarding any zoning restrictions or occupational licenses or permits you might need.

7. You're now ready to make the leap into tour leader. You'll want to stop in at various hotels, visitor centers, chambers of commerce, historical societies, and any other spots that tourists or residents might frequent to see whether you'll be able to leave promotional pamphlets on display for prospective customers. Your plan most likely will be met with enthusiasm. The above mentioned establishments are usually glad to help advertise events. Many hotels already keep racks in their lobby filled with pamphlets for various local attractions.

8. Then, prepare your pamphlets. You'll need to design and print a brochure that details your tour, how people can contact you, the times and dates you operate, and how much the tour will cost.

9. Find additional ways to promote your tour. Create a press release to send to newspapers; most papers regularly publish a calendar of events. Contact local radio stations and drop in at bookstores (a favorite hangout for mystery buffs).

10. Buy a pair of good walking shoes, dig out the sun screen, and get ready to have fun. (Panama hat is optional.)

David Kaufelt's Key West Walking Tour

In chapter 2 we met mystery writer David Kaufelt. While organizing the first Key West Literary Seminar, David put together a mystery walking tour of the island to entertain seminar participants. Here's what he has to say about the enterprise:

"Key West is the scene of many funny mysteries and murders that have never been solved. I'd been reading about them hither and yon, and I'd done some research for an article I wrote on the subject, and from that came the idea to start the mystery walking tour. We needed some money for the Key West Literary Seminar, and I thought that this would be a good way to raise some funds. We've always done a tour of great writers' houses in Key West, and the mystery tour is an offshoot of that. We do the tours when someone requests them.

"I did some research on the different houses and some of the events I knew because they happened in my time. For example, there was a huge mansion around the corner from where we used to live in Old Town. There was a young man who lived there, who no one had seen in quite some time. He'd lived with another man there, and they used to fight all the time. As it turned out, the young guy had been an alcoholic and he had died, but the older guy he lived with didn't recognize his death. He thought he was just being ornery. So he'd go get him food every day and told people how he would never speak to him, he was so ornery. But then we all started smelling something strange, and the police were finally notified. The young guy had been dead for months and had almost melted into the linoleum floor in the kitchen. The older man's mind had gone, and his family came and took him away and put him someplace.

"There's another story I like. There's an old boarding house being converted into a hotel over on Simonton Street. It used to be called the Q Rooms, and a lot of strange things happened there. One night a young guy in his twenties was walking home while the building was under construction, and he saw two pairs of legs sticking out. One pair belonged to a woman, and as he looked at the legs, he realized he knew her. She was his fiance, and she was wearing an anklet he had given her. So he pulled her out by the ankles and saw that she was dead. He pulled out the other body, who turned out to be his best friend. The couple had been making love and the 'friend' had accidentally killed her. He was alive but had passed out.

"We also go to the cemetery on the tour; there's always a funny murder there to talk about.

"If you want to start a mystery walking tour, you should do your research very well and be entertaining. You need to be able to tell an anecdote with a punch line.

"But what I would really suggest is that you try to get an organization behind you, such as Mystery Writers of America or Sisters in Crime. You could even try to find an Elder Hostel program in your area and hook up with them. People come to a city to learn, and they organize different events for them.

"You need to be in a good area to do this—Baltimore or Charleston, for example. Make sure you have something with which to identify yourself for people who will be meeting you on a street corner. It could be a T-shirt with a logo printed on it or a banner you can wave.

"And try also to get other people to share in giving the tours. After a while it can get stale."

Put Murder on the Menu

For the last ten years or so across the country, there has been a new form of entertainment especially designed to appeal to mystery buffs. No longer do restaurant goers have only their companions and food to keep them occupied. Some enterprising entrepreneurs have arranged for a waiter or waitress, a cook, or perhaps even someone dining at your table to keel over dead in front of your eyes. Shot, stabbed, or maybe even poisoned.

Whodunit? That's for diners to figure out.

If you're interested in combining your love of mystery with the drama and glamour of theater, then listen to what producer Connie Gay has to say about Murder Mystery Dinners. She and her husband Jeffrey are producers, directors, and writers for a series of shows they perform under their trademark name, MurderWatch Mystery Theater.

"About eight years ago Jeffrey and I were still living up north in Wakefield, Massachusetts, and doing legitimate theater: musicals such as *Anything Goes, Mame, Hello Dolly*, that sort of thing. We were involved with community theater and school theater; we did the acting, directing, and producing. We decided we wanted to do a different kind of theater; we were tired of doing the same old thing. So we traveled cross-country to see what was new in theater. What seemed to be pretty popular in all the major cities was mystery shows. They were what I called 'first generation' mystery shows. There would be a murder that would happen backstage. You'd be sitting in a room eating, and if you happened to be at the right table, you got the right set of clues; but if you weren't in the right location in the room, you didn't really see much of a show. We weren't really thrilled with the quality of the script of the show, but it was definitely a fun genre, we thought.

"So we discussed it on the plane ride back from our trip and decided to make it a musical mystery show. None of them had music, and that would really round out the entertainment end of it. And we wanted to make it so it was more of an environmental theater. The murder would be a theatrical spectacle. It would happen right in the room, and the body would be carried out in front of the guests. We knew that if we handled it with the right amount of humor, it wouldn't be offensive to anyone.

"We've been in Baskerville's Restaurant at the Grosvenor Resort Hotel in Lake Buena Vista, Florida, for about seven years now. The restaurant has a Sherlock Holmes theme. Every Saturday night guests get to play detective, and they also might become suspects. We make sure that there's activity in every section of the room. We make it so everyone sees something, no one sees everything, and everyone gets caught in the act."

How Connie and Jeffrey Gay Got Started

"Jeff and I went to Salem State College in Massachusetts. We were involved in theater programs there. We also had some excellent training in the high schools we went to—Jeff at Malden High, myself at Peabody High. When we graduated we were involved with Boston Globe Drama Festivals. We met during high school when he was performing at a festival and I was a judge. I had to disqualify him because his show went overtime. A year later we met again; we were both in the same class at college, and we remembered each other.

"I've been in the business since I was a child. Dancing lessons at age four, performing professionally by age nine. I had my own choreography company with which I supported myself through college.

"When we decided to do this, we looked around for a place to hold it. We've been on different cruises and in different hotels. You have to market yourself to the hotel and explain how this gimmick, so to speak, would enhance business for them.

"The Grosvenor decided to take a chance on us. Generally we pull in 150 people on a Saturday night. Sometimes more, and then we do two shows back to back.

"We also do a lot of shows on the road; we've been flown to West Virginia and Puerto Rico, for example. We do a lot of convention work and other private parties.

The Finances Involved

"When we started in the beginning, it was hard to function if we took just a cut. Some nights we'd get 150 people; some, only 80. But we still had to pay the same expenses. We agreed to charge a flat fee. The fee can vary from hotel to hotel. We pay the actors and buy our own equipment. We also have our own liability insurance.

"Jeff still keeps his day job, and I still have another part-time job. I work for the Disney University, teaching an entertainment class. We take the students around to all the theme parks at Disney and use that as our classroom.

"MurderWatch has a lot of promise, and it brings in enough to cover expenses, but it's not enough to support us right now. Nothing is easy in this business. We pay our performers on the night, but we don't always get paid on time.

"For everyone but myself this is part-time work. The actors, musicians, and technicians are all independent contractors. The work is haphazard. There's no set schedule. We rotate through about thirty different actors, musicians, and technicians. We have five different shows we do, and each one uses between eight to ten performers. I'm the only official employee.

"It's not a lucrative venture to be in any end of theater. We try to pay our performers better than average—anywhere from $50 to $100 per performance. When we're on the road, we pay their traveling expenses.

"I write all the scripts. A lot of people do call us to see if they can write for us, but what we tell them is to contact the *Blue Sheet*. There are a lot of companies that look for scripts, and they usually advertise in the *Blue Sheet*."

Pay Attention to the *Business* in *Show Business*

"Jeff and I have a lot of background in theater; we have a real solid knowledge. A lot of other groups just have a bunch of actors that get together and say, 'Let's put on a show.' Unfortunately they come and they go because they don't have solid business backgrounds. We have the business background. It is show *business* after all.

"Jeff worked for eight years in a bank and is currently working as a logistics supervisor for a major corporation. I worked eight years as a computer analyst.

"You can't organize yourself and a group of people, especially people with egos, if you don't have a solid business background.

"I also think it's important not to try to do it all yourself. Have a team of people you can trust. It doesn't have to be a big team: it could be two or three people, like with us.

"In the theater everyone becomes close and like family, and it's fun to be able to keep that atmosphere like we do, but it is a business and you can't lose sight of that fact. If you do, and you get lax, you can fail.

"We have our long-term goals, and we know where we're heading as a business. And the fun we have along the way is the fringe benefits. There's always a let's-put-on-a-show atmosphere, but we never lose sight of the bottom line."

Further Reading

The Florida Blue Sheet
7238 Hiawassee Oak Drive
Orlando, FL 32818-8360

Dale, Alzina. *Mystery Reader's Walking Guide: New York*. Lincolnwood, Ill.: NTC Publishing Group.

Dale, Alzina, and Barbara Sloan Hendershott. *Mystery Reader's Walking Guide: England*. Lincolnwood, Ill.: NTC Publishing Group.

Dale, Alzina, and Barbara Sloan Hendershott. *Mystery Reader's Walking Guide: London*. Lincolnwood, Ill.: NTC Publishing Group.

Appendix

Associations

The following list of associations can be used as a valuable resource guide in locating additional information about specific careers. Many of the organizations publish newsletters listing job and internship opportunities, and still others offer an employment service to members.

American Anthropological
    Association
1703 New Hampshire Avenue, NW
Washington, DC 20009

American Bar Association
541 North Fairbanks Court
Chicago, IL 60611-3314

American Historical Association
400 A Street, SE
Washington, DC 20003

American Library Association
50 East Huron Street
Chicago, IL 60611

American Newspaper Publishers
    Association Foundation
The Newspaper Center
Box 17407
Dulles International Airport
Washington, DC 20041

The American Newspaper
    Publishers Association
    Foundation has career
    information, including pamphlets
    titled *Newspapers: What's in It for
    me?* and *Facts about Newspapers.*

American Psychological
    Association
750 First Street, NE
Washington, DC 20002

American Society for Psychical
    Research
5 West Seventy-third Street
New York, NY 10023

American Sociological Association
1722 N Street, NW
Washington, DC 20036-2981

Archaeological Institute of
America
675 Commonwealth Avenue
Boston, MA 02215

American Society of Journalists and
Authors
1501 Broadway
New York, NY 10036

Bureau of the Census
U.S. Department of Commerce
Washington, DC 20233

Committee for the Scientific
Investigation of Claims of the
Paranormal (CSICOP)
Center for Inquiry
P.O. Box 703
Buffalo, NY 14226

The Dow Jones Newspaper Fund
P.O. Box 300
Princeton, NJ 08543-0300
The Dow Jones Newspaper Fund
offers summer reporting and
editing internships.

Genealogical Library
Church of Jesus Christ of Latter-
day Saints
Family History Library
35 North West Temple
Salt Lake City, UT 84150

Institute for Parapsychology
402 North Buchanan Boulevard
Durham, NC 27701-1728

International Union of Police
Associations
1016 Duke Street
Alexandria, VA 22314

International Security and
Detective Alliance
P.O. Box 6303
Corpus Christi, TX 78466-6303

Museum Reference Center
Office of Museum Programs
Room 2235, A&I Building
Smithsonian Institution
Washington, DC 20560

Mystery Writers of America, Inc.
Sixth Floor, 17 East Forty-seventh
Street
New York, NY 10017

National Archives
Eighth and Constitution Avenue
Washington, DC 20408

National Association of
Government Archives and
Records Administrators
c/o Director
New York State Archives
10A46 Cultural Education Center
Albany, NY 12230

National Fire Protection
Association
Batterymarch Park
Quincy, MA 02269

National Genealogical Society
4527 Seventeenth Street, N
Arlington, VA 22207-2399

National Newspaper Association
1627 K Street, NW Suite 400
Washington, DC 20006
A pamphlet titled A Career in
Newspapers can be obtained from
the National Newspaper
Association

Organization of American
   Historians
112 North Bryan Street
Bloomington, IN 47408

Sisters in Crime
P.O. Box 442124
Lawrence, KS 66044-8933

Society for American Archaeology
808 Seventeenth Street, NW
   Suite 200
Washington, DC 20006-3953

Society of American Archivists
600 South Federal Suite 504
Chicago, IL 60605

VGM CAREER BOOKS

BUSINESS PORTRAITS
Boeing
Coca-Cola
Ford
McDonald's

CAREER DIRECTORIES
Careers Encyclopedia
Dictionary of Occupational Titles
Occupational Outlook Handbook

CAREERS FOR
Animal Lovers; Bookworms; Caring
People; Computer Buffs; Crafty
People; Culture Lovers;
Environmental Types; Fashion Plates;
Film Buffs; Foreign Language
Aficionados; Good Samaritans;
Gourmets; Health Nuts; History
Buffs; Kids at Heart; Music Lovers;
Mystery Buffs; Nature Lovers; Night
Owls; Number Crunchers; Plant
Lovers; Shutterbugs; Sports Nuts;
Travel Buffs; Writers

CAREERS IN
Accounting; Advertising; Business;
Child Care; Communications;
Computers; Education; Engineering;
the Environment; Finance;
Government; Health Care; High
Tech; Horticulture & Botany;
International Business; Journalism;
Law; Marketing; Medicine; Science;
Social & Rehabilitation Services

CAREER PLANNING
Beating Job Burnout
Beginning Entrepreneur
Big Book of Jobs
Career Planning & Development for
    College Students &
    Recent Graduates
Career Change
Career Success for People with
    Physical Disabilities
Careers Checklists
College and Career Success for Students
    with Learning Disabilities
Complete Guide to Career Etiquette
Cover Letters They Don't Forget
Dr. Job's Complete Career Guide
Executive Job Search Strategies
Guide to Basic Cover Letter Writing
Guide to Basic Résumé Writing
Guide to Internet Job Searching
Guide to Temporary Employment
Job Interviewing for College Students
Joyce Lain Kennedy's Career Book

Out of Uniform
Parent's Crash Course in Career
    Planning
Slame Dunk Résumés
Up Your Grades: Proven Strategies
    for Academic Success

CAREER PORTRAITS
Animals; Cars; Computers;
Electronics; Fashion; Firefighting;
Music; Nature; Nursing; Science;
Sports; Teaching; Travel; Writing

GREAT JOBS FOR
Business Majors
Communications Majors
Engineering Majors
English Majors
Foreign Language Majors
History Majors
Psychology Majors
Sociology Majors

HOW TO
Apply to American Colleges and
    Universities
Approach an Advertising Agency and
    Walk Away with the Job You Want
Be a Super Sitter
Bounce Back Quickly After
    Losing Your Job
Change Your Career
Choose the Right Career
Cómo escribir un currículum vitae en
    inglés que tenga éxito
Find Your New Career Upon
    Retirement
Get & Keep Your First Job
Get Hired Today
Get into the Right Business School
Get into the Right Law School
Get into the Right Medical School
Get People to Do Things Your Way
Have a Winning Job Interview
Hit the Ground Running in Your
    New Job
Hold It All Together When You've
    Lost Your Job
Improve Your Study Skills
Jumpstart a Stalled Career
Land a Better Job
Launch Your Career in TV News
Make the Right Career Moves
Market Your College Degree
Move from College into a
    Secure Job
Negotiate the Raise You Deserve
Prepare Your Curriculum Vitae

Prepare for College
Run Your Own Home Business
Succeed in Advertising When all You
Succeed in College
Succeed in High School
Take Charge of Your Child's Early
    Education
Write a Winning Résumé
Write Successful Cover Letters
Write Term Papers & Reports
Write Your College Application Essay

MADE EASY
College Applications
Cover Letters
Getting a Raise
Job Hunting
Job Interviews
Résumés

**ON THE JOB: REAL PEOPLE
    WORKING IN...**
Communications
Health Care
Sales & Marketing
Service Businesses

OPPORTUNITIES IN
This extensive series provides detailed
    information on more than 150
    individual career fields.

RÉSUMÉS FOR
Advertising Careers
Architecture and Related Careers
Banking and Financial Careers
Business Management Careers
College Students &
    Recent Graduates
Communications Careers
Computer Careers
Education Careers
Engineering Careers
Environmental Careers
Ex-Military Personnel
50+ Job Hunters
Government Careers
Health and Medical Careers
High School Graduates
High Tech Careers
Law Careers
Midcareer Job Changes
Nursing Careers
Re-Entering the Job Market
Sales and Marketing Careers
Scientific and Technical Careers
Social Service Careers
The First-Time Job Hunter

 VGM Career Horizons
a division of *NTC Publishing Group*
4255 West Touhy Avenue
Lincolnwood, Illinois 60646–1975